French policemen try to hold back hordes of exuberant Parisians who filled streets, crowded onto tricolor-draped balconies and perched precariously on rooftops as General Charles de Gaulle formally ended four years of German occupation with a victory parade along the Champs-Elysées on the 26th of August, 1944.

LIBERATION

WORLD WAR II · TIME-LIFE BOOKS · ALEXANDRIA, VIRGINIA

BY MARTIN BLUMENSON
AND THE EDITORS OF TIME-LIFE BOOKS

LIBERATION

Time-Life Books Inc.
is a wholly owned subsidiary of
TIME INCORPORATED

Founder: Henry R. Luce 1898-1967

Editor-in-Chief: Henry Anatole Grunwald
Chairman of the Board: Andrew Heiskell
President: James R. Shepley
Editorial Director: Ralph Graves
Vice Chairman: Arthur Temple

TIME-LIFE BOOKS INC.

Managing Editor: Jerry Korn
Executive Editor: David Maness
Assistant Managing Editors: Dale M. Brown
(planning), George Constable, George G. Daniels
(acting), Martin Mann, John Paul Porter
Art Director: Tom Suzuki
Chief of Research: David L. Harrison
Director of Photography: Robert G. Mason
Senior Text Editor: Diana Hirsh
Assistant Art Director: Arnold C. Holeywell
Assistant Chief of Research: Carolyn L. Sackett
Assistant Director of Photography: Dolores A. Littles

Chairman: Joan D. Manley
President: John D. McSweeney
Executive Vice Presidents: Carl G. Jaeger,
John Steven Maxwell, David J. Walsh
Vice Presidents: George Artandi (comptroller);
Stephen L. Bair (legal counsel); Peter G. Barnes;
Nicholas Benton (public relations);
John L. Canova; Beatrice T. Dobie (personnel);
Carol Flaumenhaft (consumer affairs);
Nicholas J. C. Ingleton (Asia); James L. Mercer
(Europe/South Pacific); Herbert Sorkin
(production); Paul R. Stewart (marketing)

WORLD WAR II

Editorial Staff for *Liberation*
Editor: William K. Goolrick
Picture Editor/Designer: Raymond Ripper
Text Editors: Gerald Simons, Henry Woodhead
Staff Writers: Dalton Delan, Malachy J. Duffy,
Brian McGinn, Tyler Mathisen,
Teresa M. C. R. Pruden
Chief Researcher: Frances G. Youssef
Researchers: Michael Blumenthal,
Loretta Y. Britten, Josephine Burke,
Christine Bowie Dove, Jane Edwin,
Frances R. Glennon, Oobie Gleysteen, Pat Good,
Catherine Gregory, Chadwick Gregson,
Clara Nicolai
Art Assistant: Mary Louise Mooney
Editorial Assistant: Connie Strawbridge

Editorial Production
Production Editor: Douglas B. Graham
Operations Manager: Gennaro C. Esposito,
Gordon E. Buck (assistant)
Assistant Production Editor: Feliciano Madrid
Quality Control: Robert L. Young (director),
James J. Cox (assistant), Daniel J. McSweeney,
Michael G. Wight (associates)
Art Coordinator: Anne B. Landry
Copy Staff: Susan B. Galloway (chief),
Patricia Graber, Victoria Lee, Celia Beattie
Picture Department: Alvin L. Ferrell

Correspondents: Elisabeth Kraemer (Bonn);
Margot Hapgood, Dorothy Bacon, Lesley Coleman
(London); Susan Jonas, Lucy T. Voulgaris (New
York); Maria Vincenza Aloisi, Josephine du Brusle
(Paris); Ann Natanson (Rome). Valuable assistance
was also provided by: Janny Hovinga (Hilversum,
Netherlands); Judy Aspinall (London); Carolyn T.
Chubet, Miriam Hsia, Christina Lieberman (New
York); John Scott (Ottawa, Ontario); M. T.
Hirschkoff (Paris); Mimi Murphy (Rome).

The Author: MARTIN BLUMENSON, educated at
Bucknell and Harvard, served in the U.S. Army in
World War II as historical officer with the Third
and Seventh Armies in the European Theater of
Operations. Later, he commanded the 3rd Histori-
cal Detachment in Korea and was the Historian of
Joint Task Force Seven during atomic weapons
tests in the Pacific. He has been a visiting professor
at Acadia University, The Citadel, and the Army
and Naval War Colleges. Among his books are
*Breakout and Pursuit; Anzio: The Gamble That
Failed; Kasserine Pass; Salerno to Cassino; The
Patton Papers, 1885-1940* and *1940-1945;* and *The
Vilde Affair: Beginnings of the French Resistance.*

The Consultants: COL. JOHN R. ELTING, USA
(Ret.) is a military historian and author of *The
Battle of Bunker's Hill; The Battles of Saratoga;* and
Military History and Atlas of the Napoleonic Wars.
He edited *Military Uniforms in America: The Era
of the American Revolution, 1755-1795* and *Mili-
tary Uniforms in America: Years of Growth, 1796-
1851,* and was associate director of *The West Point
Atlas of American Wars.*

CHARLES B. MACDONALD is the Deputy Chief
Historian for Southeast Asia in the U.S. Army Center of Military History. He served as a rifle company commander in the 2nd Infantry Division during World War II, and was awarded the Silver Star
and the Purple Heart. His books include: *The Siegfried Line Campaign; The Last Offensive; Company Commander; The Battle of the Huertgen Forest; Airborne* (a history of airborne operations in
World War II); and *The Mighty Endeavor: American Armed Forces in the European Theater in
World War II.*

Library of Congress Cataloguing in Publication Data

Blumenson, Martin.
    Liberation.

    (World War II; v. 14)
    Bibliography: p.
    Includes index.
    1. World War, 1939-1945—Campaigns—France—
Normandy. 2. World War, 1939-1945—France—Paris. 3.
Paris—History—1940-1944. I. Time-Life Books. II. Title.
III. Series.
D756.5.N6B57   940.54'21   78-21967
ISBN 0-8094-2512-2
ISBN 0-8094-2511-4 lib. bdg.

For information about any Time-Life book, please write:

Reader Information
Time-Life Books
541 North Fairbanks Court
Chicago, Illinois 60611

CHAPTERS

PICTURE ESSAYS

CONTENTS

PARIS UNDER THE SWASTIKA

Led by a spit-and-polish military band, German security troops strut down the Champs-Elysées at noontime in a daily ritual most Parisians deliberately ignored.

GALLIC ESPRIT VS. THE THIRD REICH

By the summer of 1944, when the Allies were attempting to break out of their Normandy beachhead, France had been under the German yoke for four years. The Occupation was oppressive in every region of the country. Germans searched houses and arrested innocent civilians, rationed food and fuel, carted off valuables and deported young men to work in German war industries. But nowhere was the German presence more acutely felt or bitterly resented than in Paris—the country's capital and the city that symbolized France to most Frenchmen.

An occupation force of more than 30,000 administrative and security troops moved into the city, took over 500 hotels and hung huge swastikas from public buildings and monuments. The Germans reserved the best restaurants for their officers and set aside cinemas and brothels for their soldiers. They outraged Parisians by parading troops and bands through the city, by naming streets after German heroes and by melting down 200 of Paris' statues for bronze.

In addition to flaunting their victory with banners and bands, the Germans intimidated Parisians with hundreds of humiliating regulations and restrictions. Displaying the national tricolor or singing the "Marseillaise" was forbidden. Anyone who insulted a German soldier, defaced a propaganda poster or listened to BBC broadcasts was subject to arrest and imprisonment. Public gatherings and demonstrations were controlled, and a strictly enforced curfew kept Parisians at home from midnight to 5:30 a.m.

In their daily contacts with Parisians, the Germans were ordered to behave correctly and courteously. They usually were careful to pay for everything they bought. They used German-French phrase books to try to engage the French people in friendly conversations. But their efforts made little difference to most Parisians, especially those whose husbands, brothers, sons or fathers were among the two million French prisoners of war in Germany. When a visiting German wondered what had happened to the city's gaiety and *joie de vivre,* a Parisian bitterly responded: "You should have come when you were not here."

German road signs, located at major Paris intersections such as the Place de l'Opéra, guided drivers to military headquarters and support units.

LE MARÉCHAL Remercie les Légionnaires de leur Message
« En participant à la croisade dont l'Allemagne a pris la tête, acquérant ainsi de justes titres à la reconnaissance du monde, vous contribuez à écarter de nous le péril bolchevique »

Under a giant poster of Marshal Pétain, head of the French puppet government at Vichy, Parisians read clippings from a German-controlled newspaper.

Accompanied by a smartly dressed friend, Luftwaffe officers study the odds at the Auteuil race track, where underfed horses ran during the Occupation.

At a Paris bookstall, a soldier finds a German title among the French and English ones. Newsstands sold a daily paper and dozens of magazines in German.

German soldiers jostle past civilians to inspect the wares at the Paris Flea Market. Merchants routinely overcharged the Germans for perfumes and trinkets.

Outside a military barracks in Paris, German soldiers and band members await a formal inspection.

Oblivious of a nearby cinema for German soldiers, Parisians crowd around a street peddler's table.

From his headquarters in the swastika-bedecked

TURNING A COLD SHOULDER TO THE ENEMY

Using the ancient strategy of dividing and conquering, the Germans turned French against French and created an atmosphere of fear and suspicion among Parisians. The chief architects of this policy were the Ge-

Hôtel Meurice, the German military commander of Paris issued orders to his garrison and controlled every detail of the daily lives of three million Parisians.

stapo and SS, which recruited waiters, servants and concierges into a network of informers and offered cash rewards for reports of hostile actions or attitudes. Some Parisians took advantage of the offer to settle grudges against former business associates or lovers, and a daily stream of anonymous denunciations flowed into Gestapo headquarters on the Avenue Foch.

Thousands of Parisians were dragged out of their homes in the small hours of the morning and whisked away by the Gestapo. Some were guilty of nothing more than an anti-German remark. Some were tortured and released with a warning that worse would follow if they talked about their treatment; many were deported to prison camps and never heard of again.

To protect themselves from this reign of terror, Parisians repressed their feelings and hid their true opinions with noncommittal comments or complete silence. No one discussed politics in public, and the people went to such lengths to avoid eye contact that the Germans nicknamed Paris *la ville sans regard* (roughly, "the city that never looks at you").

13

At the Berlitz language school, the Germans opened an anti-Semitic exhibit entitled "The Jew and France" in September 1941. Indoors, a bust with exaggerated racial features illustrated how to recognize Jews, graphic displays chronicled Jewish "misdeeds" and posters depicted the Jews' allegedly pernicious influence on French politics and culture.

THE SIGNS OF HATRED

In addition to the restrictions and privations imposed on their fellow Parisians, the 160,000 Jewish residents of Paris were subjected to the brutal excesses of Hitler's racial policies. French Jews were virtual prisoners in their native city. Their businesses were confiscated, their homes looted of valuables, and many were forbidden to practice their professions. They were forced to wear yellow stars on their clothing and were banned from restaurants, markets, parks and phone booths.

Stateless, foreign-born Jews living in Paris suffered a more brutal fate. They were the targets of frequent SS-organized roundups, and more than 30,000 were deported to concentration camps. Of the almost 13,000 non-French Jews arrested in July 1942, only 30 survived the horrors of Auschwitz.

Wearing the required yellow star with the word "Juif" (Jew) in the center, a Jewish

woman grimly goes about her business. Non-Jewish Parisians ridiculed the German regulation by wearing stars with such inscriptions as "Buddhist" and "Zulu."

1

When the Allied armies landed in Normandy on June 6, 1944, they expected to make rapid progress once they were safely on shore. Preinvasion plans called for the British to take the critical road junction at Caen and push inland 20 miles the first day. At the opposite end of the line, American forces were supposed to cut across the Cotentin Peninsula, turn north and take the great port of Cherbourg by D-plus-8. In the area between these two critical objectives, American troops were expected to push southward into Normandy and establish themselves on an east-west line running through Saint-Lô and Caumont—approximately 16 miles inland—by D-plus-9.

Once these objectives were attained, the plan called for Allied forces to sweep through the entire Brittany peninsula, capture the port of Brest and seize a large area between the Loire and the Seine Rivers. By the end of three months, an avalanche of supplies, weapons and troops would be pouring into the beachhead, and the Allies would be in possession of a giant springboard for a massive drive across northern France toward Germany. Meanwhile, plans were afoot for a large-scale invasion of France's Mediterranean coast; the Allied forces landed there were to drive north up the Rhone Valley and join with the eastbound forces from Normandy, thereby trapping all the German troops in southwestern France in the jaws of a giant pincers and completing the liberation of France. Then the final defeat of the German armies and the end of the War might be within the Allies' grasp.

But by the middle of June, the expansion of the Normandy beachhead had fallen behind the timetable set by the planners. Caen was still in German hands, and Allied forces were nowhere near Cherbourg. They had pushed isolated salients down to Villers Bocage and Caumont, but they were stymied on the way to Saint-Lô, and along most of the rest of the front the offensive had slowed to a crawl.

There were two major reasons why the Allied advance had bogged down: the tenacity of the Germans and their skillful use of the terrain. As the Germans faced north toward the sea, they could see that the mortal threat to their forces lay in the Caen area at the eastern end of the front. The country was wide open there, ideally suited for tank operations. Beyond Caen, gently rolling hills led toward Falaise and the heart of France. A breakthrough in this area

BATTLE OF THE HEDGEROWS

could spell disaster for the Germans, posing the threat of encirclement of all their divisions in Normandy and undermining their whole defensive position in the West. Accordingly, the Germans deployed the majority of their forces in the area of Caen and ferociously resisted every attempt by the British to capture the city and break into the plains that lay beyond.

West of Caen the terrain was made to order for the defense, and the Germans could afford to spread their forces more thinly. This was the hedgerow country, or *bocage* as the French called it—a patchwork of thousands of small fields enclosed by almost impenetrable hedges. The hedges consisted of dense thickets of hawthorn, brambles, vines and trees ranging up to 15 feet in height, growing out of earthen mounds several feet thick and three or four feet high, with a drainage ditch on either side. The walls and hedges together were so formidable that each field took on the character of a small fort. Defenders dug in at the base of a hedgerow and hidden by vegetation were all but impervious to rifle and artillery fire. So dense was the vegetation that infantrymen poking around the hedgerows sometimes found themselves staring eye to eye at startled Germans. A single machine gun concealed in a hedgerow could mow down attacking troops as they attempted to advance from one hedge to another. Snipers, mounted on wooden platforms in the treetops and using flashless gunpowder to avoid giving away their positions, were a constant threat.

Most of the roads were wagon trails, worn into sunken lanes by centuries of use and turned into cavern-like mazes by overarching hedges. These gloomy passages were tailor made for ambushes and were terrifying places for men on both sides. "In a sunken road," Corporal John Welch of the Seaforth Highlanders later said, "the tension left me feeling like a wet rag."

The sunken lanes were also deathtraps for tanks. Confined to narrow channels, they were easy marks for German *Panzerfausts*—antitank rocket launchers—camouflaged in the hedgerows. A tank that ventured off the road and attempted to smash through the thicket was particularly vulnerable. As it climbed the mound at the base of the hedgerow, its guns were pointed helplessly skyward and its underbelly was exposed to fire from antitank guns in the next hedgerow. Dennis Bunn of the Scottish 15th Recon-

naissance Regiment, who fought in the hedgerows, described what it was like to drive through them in a heavy armored car. "Inside the car was intense heat and darkness, outside brilliant sunshine. I sweated and gripped the steering wheel with damp hands as I peered through a small aperture at the ground in front, the high hedge on the right, the ground sloping away to the left, at the trees, the bushes, seeing or suspecting danger in every blade of grass."

The mental and physical strain were so exhausting that discipline was affected. There was a great deal of drinking—this was Calvados country—but with or without the assistance of alcohol, many men seemed to be in a stupor. "Over a stretch of time," said an American platoon leader, "you became so dulled by fatigue that the names of the killed and wounded they checked off each night, the names of men who had been your best friends, might have come out of a telephone book for all you knew. All the old values were gone, and if there was a world beyond this tangle of hedgerows you never expected to live to see it."

The weather compounded the soldiers' miseries. Through much of June and the first half of July, a cold, clammy rain fell, turning the earth into a quagmire. Fighting from field to field, troops crawled and slogged through pelting rain and ankle-deep water. The sickly sweet smell of death assaulted their nostrils. And every so often they came upon the grim spectacle of hastily improvised graves topped with crude wooden crosses, boltless rifles or steel helmets.

The Germans fought with great stubbornness and skill in the hedgerow country, although weeks after the landings Hitler and his generals were still not ready to concede that this was the main Allied attack. They persisted in their belief that the major effort would come in the Pas-de-Calais area, up the coast of France from Normandy. And while the fighting raged in Normandy, they kept the Fifteenth Army —some 200,000 men strong—guarding the Calais coast against an attack that would never come.

Nevertheless, the Führer viewed the Normandy invasion as a threat that must be eliminated at all costs. He told his top subordinates in the West—the respected Field Marshals Gerd von Rundstedt, the theater commander, and Erwin Rommel, the commander of Army Group B—that "every man shall fight and die where he stands." Even though the units in the Pas-de-Calais area remained untouchable, Hitler directed that seven other divisions be transferred to the battle area from Brittany, the Bay of Biscay area, central, eastern and southern France, and from as far away as the Eastern Front. If the Allied armies could be confined to a small area close to the English Channel, he believed that a decisive counterstroke could still be launched. The beaches could be regained, and the Allies could be sent reeling back into the sea.

Meanwhile, the Allies were concocting a plan of attack of their own that called for a one-two punch against the Germans. The British under Lieut. General Sir Miles Dempsey would strike at Caen and attack the bulk of the enemy's forces. And while the British Second Army "got the enemy by the throat," as General Dwight D. Eisenhower, the Su-

preme Allied Commander, put it, the American First Army would push north to take the port of Cherbourg.

The Caen attack had to be put off because of a shortage of ammunition, but on the 14th of June, American troops set out to capture Cherbourg. The U.S. First Army commander, Lieut. General Omar N. Bradley, planned the offensive in two basic stages, using the VII Corps under Major General J. Lawton Collins as his spearhead. Collins would drive westward 20 miles from the road junction at Carentan to the west coast of the Cotentin Peninsula. Then the American force would change direction and push northward toward Cherbourg.

Collins, who had earned his spurs as a division commander on Guadalcanal, launched the attack with two of the U.S. Army's most reliable divisions, the 82nd Airborne and the

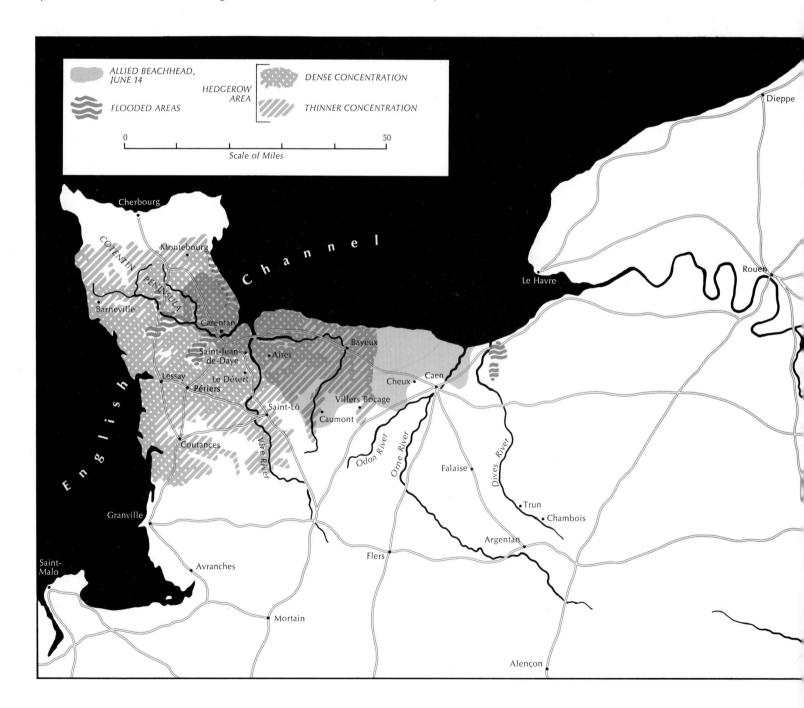

9th Infantry. As they headed westward from Carentan they had to cross the Merderet and Douve Rivers, both of which were flanked by huge marshes. Normally, most of the area drained sufficiently in the summertime to be used as grazing land for cattle, but by mid-1944 the Germans had constructed concrete dams that kept the fields flooded, which restricted all movement to causeways and footpaths. The American troops had to force their way along these narrow passages under heavy enemy fire.

But the Germans had their own problems. They were short of ammunition, and the only tanks available to them in this sector were obsolete French models that had fallen into German hands after the debacle of 1940. As Collins delivered a series of sharp infantry jabs on a narrow front, the Germans pulled back. In the process they split their

forces, most of them turning south on the coast road, and the rest retreating north to help defend Cherbourg.

Near Barneville-sur-Mer on the morning of the 18th of June, American artillery caught part of the southbound force, a column attempting to escape down the coastal highway, and methodically destroyed it, littering the road with wrecked vehicles. The Cotentin Peninsula was now cut off, and the stage was set for an attack to the north to capture the port of Cherbourg. Before this attack could get under way, American forces were regrouped and reorganized. Collins was given the 4th, 9th and 79th Infantry Divisions for the attack to the north. The recently activated VIII Corps—with the 90th Infantry Division and the 82nd and 101st Airborne Divisions—was given the assignment of holding a defensive line across the peninsula to protect the rear of Collins' troops.

As the men of Collins' VII Corps started for Cherbourg, they were held up briefly by enemy troops dug in along a railroad embankment in the Montebourg area. But the opposition was merely a gesture. The commander of the Cherbourg garrison, Lieut. General Karl Wilhelm von Schlieben, was under orders from Hitler to carry out a fighting withdrawal, then to hold Cherbourg at all costs. Schlieben just wanted to show that he was obeying the Führer's command. That night he drew his forces back into a system of forts and strong points protecting the port from the landward side.

On June 20 the three American divisions ran into this defensive complex, a belt of steel and concrete fortifications arranged in a semicircle four to six miles south of the city. Massive blockhouses were spotted along the perimeter; they had underground ammunition storage bunkers connected by trenches, and the area around the blockhouses was interlaced with barbed wire and crisscrossed by antitank ditches. Bristling with automatic weapons and covered by artillery, the bunkers commanded every approach to the city. It quickly became clear that there would be no easy entry into Cherbourg. When one battalion attempted to move past a crossroad on the edge of the city, machine guns opened up from houses all around. A deluge of artillery shells from nearby hills struck the command group, mortally wounding the battalion commander, injuring his staff and driving the whole unit back. Another battalion, attacking a suburb of Cherbourg, was hit by small-arms fire

Before the Allies could break out of the Normandy beachhead and liberate France, they had to overcome a stubborn German defense in some of Western Europe's most difficult terrain, the hedgerows of Normandy. Varying in concentration as indicated by the density of the lines on the map, the hedgerows provided ideal defensive positions for the enemy. The Germans made Allied progress all the more arduous by flooding large areas through the manipulation of dams they had built for this purpose. But by the middle of July, American forces had reached Saint-Lô and, with British troops near Caen, the Allies were poised for the major offensive that eventually would drive the Germans from France.

and shellfire; within just a few minutes 31 men were dead and 92 injured.

Inside Cherbourg, notwithstanding the spirited defense encountered by U.S. troops on the outer fringes, all was not well. Schlieben had about 25,000 men at his disposal, but they were of doubtful fighting quality. Included were policemen, Naval personnel assigned to port duties, clerks, antiaircraft gunners and slave laborers from all over the Continent who had been brought in to work on fortifications and V-1 missile sites. Of the combat troops, one fifth were non-German: Poles, Russian and Italians swept into the German war machine as a by-product of conquest and occupation. The defenders were further handicapped by a shortage of weapons and supplies. Though the garrison had been doubled since before D-Day, the Cherbourg area had never been adequately provisioned for a siege. Now there was not enough time to correct the shortages of food, fuel and ammunition.

Hitler himself was apprehensive. "Even if worse comes to worst," he informed Schlieben, "it is your duty to defend the last bunker and leave the enemy not a harbor but a field of ruins." Schlieben replied forlornly that his garrison was totally exhausted, had been trained poorly and included too many older men.

Collins had hoped to avoid a frontal assault against the city. But he was growing more and more impatient—a restless figure in a trench coat stalking the front lines. On June 21 he directed that an ultimatum be broadcast to the defenders in German, Polish and French, threatening them with annihilation if they did not surrender by 9 o'clock the next morning. But with Hitler breathing down his neck, Schlieben was in no mood to capitulate. Instead, he gave his troops a terse order. "Withdrawal from present positions is punishable by death," he said. "I empower all leaders of whatever rank to shoot at sight anyone who leaves his post because of cowardice."

When his ultimatum expired without an answer, Collins called for an "air pulverization" of the fortifications. On the afternoon of June 22, four squadrons of RAF Typhoons —rocket-firing fighter-bombers—spewed their deadly ordnance into the fortress. Six squadrons of RAF Mustangs then strafed the German defenses, and 375 U.S. fighter-bombers attacked in waves at five-minute intervals, bombing and strafing the area for an hour. The result was a spectacular show, but not an unmixed success. The fortifications were a long way from being pulverized, and some American troops were strafed by their own planes. But the bombing did further sap the garrison's already weakened morale, and in ground attacks on June 23, all three U.S. divisions made significant headway against the main German defenses.

Schlieben now reported to Rommel and Hitler that the fall of Cherbourg was only a matter of time. Pointing out that there were 2,000 wounded troops in the city who could not be cared for adequately with available medical supplies, he asked whether the destruction of his force was really necessary. He was told to keep fighting.

On June 25, as the Americans tightened their grip on Cherbourg, troops of the 79th Division came up against Fort du Roule, the strongest of all of the city's defensive positions. Built into the face of a promontory, the multilevel fort afforded protection against attack by sea or land. Heavy coastal guns, under the edge of a cliff, commanded Cherbourg's harbor, while machine guns and mortars in concrete pillboxes atop the promontory pointed in the opposite direction to stave off attackers from the landward side. The approaches to this bristling complex of fortifications were covered by a large antitank ditch, barbed-wire entanglements and bunkers. On the sloping ground at the base of the promontory, infantrymen were deeply entrenched.

As the troops of the 79th struggled forward, they came under heavy machine-gun and mortar fire from the top of the promontory. German artillery zeroed in on them, and a hail of small-arms fire poured down from the infantry entrenched on the slope.

While an artillery battalion of the 79th Division took the fort under fire, all of the machine guns of two infantry battalions were trained on the German infantrymen. Inch by inch the attackers worked their way toward the fort, covering each short advance with small-arms and machine-gun fire, blasting gaps in the wire with Bangalore torpedoes, planting demolitions in pillboxes and blowing them up. To flush out the defenders, they combined pole charges —demolitions attached to the ends of long rods—with "beehives," packets of explosives covered with an adhesive substance that stuck to pillboxes and other fortifications.

A MOSAIC OF FORTIFIED FIELDS AND DEATHTRAPS THAT STALLED AN ARMY

An aerial photograph reveals the Normandy countryside as a mosaic divided by hedgerows into hundreds of small, tightly enclosed fields.

Normandy's hedgerows, compact earthen mounds covered with thornbush and trees and encompassing an average of 500 small fields per square mile, stretched before the Allied invaders like a never-ending obstacle course, 60 miles long and 25 miles wide. Intended originally to mark property boundaries and to shield crops from violent sea winds, the hedgerows afforded near-perfect concealment for German rifles, mortars, machine guns and antitank weapons. And they were all but insuperable barriers for Allied tanks.

Armored units began a desperate search for a device that could blast or cut its way through the obstacles. The breakthrough was achieved when Sergeant Curtis G. Culin Jr. of the U.S. 102nd Cavalry Reconnaissance Squadron welded pointed steel blades cut from German beach obstacles to a tank, enabling it to plow through the hedgerows with guns blazing. Culin's invention worked so well that General Bradley had "hedgerow cutters" mounted on three of every five tanks in the First Army. General Eisenhower later wrote that these ingenious devices "restored the effectiveness of the tank and gave a tremendous boost to morale throughout the Army."

Armed with steel blades, a light tank prepares to slice through a hedge.

Searching a hedgerow for snipers, soldiers advance past a dead comrade.

In one area of the front, Corporal John D. Kelly and his platoon of the 314th Infantry Regiment were pinned down by fire from a pillbox. Kelly crawled back to the rear to get a pole charge. Then he advanced up the slope under fire to the base of the pillbox, set the charge and exploded it at the end of the pole. But the explosion had no effect; machine guns in the pillbox went right on firing. Kelly slithered back down the hill as bullets whined around him, got another charge, crawled up the slope again and managed to blow off the ends of the machine guns that were sticking out of the pillbox slits. Still the pillbox defenders refused to yield. Kelly went back down the hill and repeated the whole process. This time he blew the rear door of the pillbox open. Then he flung some grenades through the doorway, and the survivors came out and surrendered.

By midnight on June 25, men of the 79th Division had cleared the upper defenses of Fort du Roule. The following day, tanks and tank destroyers fired armor-piercing shells at the face of the promontory. A demolition team lowered charges from above the fort, and an assault team finally climbed the promontory to rout the last of the defenders.

The end was now clearly in sight at Cherbourg. Schlieben tried to bolster the sagging spirits of his troops by handing out Iron Crosses that were dropped in by parachute. But he could see that the garrison was doomed. "I must state in the line of duty," he radioed to Rommel, "that further sacrifices cannot alter anything." Rommel reminded him of the Führer's order to fight to the end. Schlieben took over personal command of the fighting around his command post. Forced finally to retreat to his underground bunker headquarters, he radioed his last message: "Documents burned, codes destroyed."

From a prisoner the Americans learned where Schlieben was holed up. On June 26 two rifle companies worked their way toward the command shelter and sent a prisoner in through the tunnel entrance to demand the German commander's surrender. When Schlieben refused, tank destroyers were summoned to fire into the tunnel. A few rounds flushed out some 800 defenders, including the commander. Four hundred Germans preparing to defend the city hall gave themselves up once they were convinced that Schlieben had been captured.

The surrender of Cherbourg threw Hitler into a rage; he had expected Schlieben to defend the city until he and everyone else was killed. Schlieben later blamed the troops. Their "fighting ability," he wrote, "can only be described as inferior." He added: "You can't expect Russians and Poles to fight for Germany against Americans in France."

By the last day of June, two weeks behind schedule, Cherbourg was in American hands, and the 9th Division was mopping up the remaining enemy defenders on nearby Cap de la Hague. But for the time being the coveted port was an empty prize. The Germans had surrendered, but they had effectively denied the Allies the harbor. The architect of the destruction, Rear Admiral Walther Hennecke, was captured with Schlieben, but he was awarded the Knight's Cross by Hitler, who called the admiral's feat "unprecedented in the annals of coastal defense."

The port was a shambles. Mines were everywhere. Sunken ships blocked all the basins. The harbor's electrical system and dock machinery were destroyed. Quay walls were damaged, cranes were toppled and twisted, the breakwater was so heavily cratered that the sea washed through it. Three weeks of intensive clearing would be needed before the port could begin to operate. Not until September would all the obstructions be removed. Meanwhile, the bulk of supplies for the Allied troops on the Continent must continue to come in over the Normandy beaches.

On June 20 Hitler ordered the first move in his campaign to drive the Allies back into the sea. He called for a massive counterattack at the end of June aimed at Bayeux, near the hinge between the American First and the British Second Armies. In the attack the 2nd Panzer Corps, consisting of two seasoned armored divisions from the Eastern Front, would combine with two other divisions in reserve and two already in line in Normandy.

There was only one problem: the 2nd Panzer had to get there. Allied fighter-bombers and the French Resistance had so crippled the transportation network that the panzer corps—not to mention critically needed supplies—was prevented from reaching the front. Before it could arrive, the British beat the Germans to the punch.

Two days before Hitler issued his attack order, General Sir Bernard L. Montgomery, Allied ground forces commander, had written his own directive for an attack on Caen, code-named *Epsom*. General Dempsey's Second Army was ordered to encircle the city; the main effort would be made by the VIII Corps, under Lieut. General Sir Richard O'Connor, a veteran of the fighting in the North African desert who had been captured by the Italians in Libya in 1941 and released a few days after Italy's capitulation in September 1943. The attack was to involve 60,000 troops, 600 tanks and 300 guns, plus the support of 400 artillery pieces from adjacent corps areas and additional backup from naval gun-

fire and air power. O'Connor's mission was to cross the Odon River and take the high ground south of Caen.

The troops committed to *Epsom* were largely untried, but they went at it with a vengeance. Part of the attacking force was the 49th Division, whose men had served as an occupation force in Iceland and were known as the "Polar Bears." The division jumped off early on the morning of June 25 in a heavy mist. Machine-gun and tank fire from the Germans mowed down many attackers, but the survivors closed with

After surrendering to an officer of the U.S. 9th Division, Lieut. General Karl Wilhelm von Schlieben (center), commander of Cherbourg, and Rear Admiral Walther Hennecke (in visored cap, right), Naval commander in Normandy, are escorted to American Army headquarters on June 26, 1944. Although later denounced by Hitler as a poor commander, Schlieben held off U.S. forces long enough for Hennecke to demolish the city's port facilities. Schlieben turned himself over to the Americans in order to save the lives of some 300 wounded soldiers who shared his underground shelter with him and were suffocating from noxious artillery fumes.

the enemy and fought with such fury that they later were called the "Butcher Bears."

The British attack inched ahead as O'Connor unleashed an entire armored division on a narrow front. The tank column was supposed to punch through to the corps' objectives across the Odon River. But the tanks got stalled in the wreckage of the heavily bombarded town of Cheux, and German artillery forced the supporting infantry to dig in. A heavy rain started to fall, miring both the British and the German armor.

During the next couple of days, the VIII Corps managed to seize a bridgehead across the Odon and to get some tanks onto high ground beyond the river. But Montgomery and Dempsey had begun to worry about concentrations of German armor reported by aerial reconnaissance and about plans for the Bayeux counterattack found on a captured SS officer. They decided to break off the British offensive and consolidate their positions in readiness for a German blow. It proved to be a wise decision.

The blow fell on June 29, and the British were prepared. Six German panzer divisions spearheading the attack were blasted by British antitank guns and by a tremendous sea and air bombardment. Even the near misses from 16-inch naval shells knocked out Panther and Tiger tanks, blowing them over on their sides like toys. Heavy bombers struck the town of Villers Bocage, creating such rubble that German tanks could not move through it for the attack.

Under the ferocious British pounding, the force of the German effort spent itself in a single day. Rommel's headquarters recorded a "complete defensive success"—the attack on Caen had been stymied—but that was not what the Führer had in mind. The German Seventh Army had expended the forces being assembled for the climactic thrust at Bayeux that was supposed to knock the Allied troops back into the sea.

Rundstedt and Rommel were convinced in any case that the Germans could never regain the initiative. On the day that O'Connor launched his attack, they had recommended going over to the defensive as a matter of policy, "no matter how undesirable this may be," as Rundstedt phrased it. When Hitler met with his top commanders at his Bavarian mountain eyrie at Berchtesgaden on June 29, Rommel proposed that a new defensive line be established along the Seine. He noted that the latest British offensive had been stopped only by the commitment of the force allocated for the Bayeux push.

Hitler responded with a harangue: the panzers should have "Dunkirked" the British. Coupled with the onslaught of V-1 missiles then in progress against London, the attack could have forced the British to sue for peace. The Germans were still capable of offensive action, the Führer declared—dependent, of course, "on when troops and supplies can be brought up." In any event, the Allies seemed incapable of breaking out of their beachhead, and no ground must be yielded to them under any circumstances. There was to be no thought of strategic withdrawal. "We must not allow mobile warfare to develop," Hitler said, "because the enemy surpasses us by far in mobility. . . . Therefore everything depends on fighting a war of attrition to wear him down and force him back."

Depressed by the Führer's rantings, Rundstedt and Rommel returned to France. The situation was now deteriorating rapidly, with German casualties outnumbering replacements. German vehicles needed 200,000 more gallons of fuel per day than were available. Other supplies also fell far short of the need. Only 400 tons of supplies were reaching the front every day through the crippled transportation system; 2,250 tons were required.

On July 1, with a steady rain falling and Allied fighter-bombers grounded, the German Seventh Army launched another attack in an effort to wipe out the British salient across the Odon River. The attack was stopped cold—mainly by massive concentrations of artillery. Rundstedt saw the failure as further evidence of the futility of the German effort. He called Field Marshal Wilhelm Keitel, chief of the OKW, the German Armed Forces High Command, and explained the situation to him.

"What shall we do? What shall we do?" asked the distraught Keitel.

"Make peace, you fools," Rundstedt answered. "What else can you do?"

Keitel reported the conversation to Hitler, and the next day the Führer's adjutant arrived at Rundstedt's headquarters in Saint-Germain-en-Laye, just outside of Paris, and gave Rundstedt the oak leaf cluster to the Knight's Cross and a polite handwritten message from Hitler that removed him from command.

Rundstedt was supplanted by Field Marshal Günther von Kluge. Valued by Hitler as a general who obeyed orders and kept his mouth shut, Kluge had led the German drive to the Channel in 1940 and had served on the Russian front before taking over in the West. In assuming his new command, he announced his commitment to an "unconditional holding of the present defense line."

Available for this assignment were the Seventh Army under General Paul Hausser and the Panzer Group West led by Lieut. General Heinrich Eberbach. Together these forces comprised six corps and nearly 500 tanks. The bulk of the men and all but about 70 tanks were positioned south of Caen, organized in depth along three defensive lines to protect the Falaise plain. The remainder guarded the American sector south of the Cotentin Peninsula, where the combination of hedgerows and marshes favored the defense.

On July 4, Dempsey launched an attack aimed at taking Caen once and for all. The battle opened with the Canadians of the 3rd Infantry Division—supported by flamethrowing tanks, 428 field guns and the 16-inch guns of battleships in the Channel—driving for the airfield at Carpiquet, next door to Caen. On the first day the Canadians took the village of Carpiquet and the hangars on the northern edge of the airfield. The southern half of the field remained in enemy hands. The 12th SS Panzer (Hitler Jugend) Division, a unit of teenagers who made up for their youthfulness by the fierceness with which they fought, launched a series of counterattacks on July 5. Some of the Canadian positions were penetrated, but the enemy attacks were beaten off by artillery and RAF fighter-bombers.

The airfield was still in German hands on July 7, when the main attack on Caen was set in motion. Three divisions, 115,000 men, pushed off toward the northern suburbs of Caen after an overwhelming air and artillery preparation.

Pinned down amid the rubble of La Bijude, two and a half miles north of Caen, members of the British I Corps' 59th Division protect their comrades with rifle fire as they dash for a doorway. Delayed by street fighting that cost the 59th Division more than 1,000 casualties, the drive on Caen took the Allies 33 more days than D-Day planners had expected.

HITLER'S FANTASTIC FLYING WEAPONS

In a last-ditch attempt to break the morale of Allied civilians in Europe, Hitler during the summer of 1944 unleashed more than 10,000 jet- and rocket-propelled bombs against population centers, primarily London. The Germans called their two new missiles V-1 and V-2; the V stood for *Vergeltungswaffen*—retaliation weapons.

The jet-powered V-1 killed more than 6,000 and wounded over 17,000 just in the London area. However, the noisy V-1 was plagued by a relatively slow speed—400 mph, which enabled British air defenses to shoot down many of the missiles—and by a faulty guidance system.

Much more deadly—although perhaps not as frightening because it approached in silence—was the V-2, a 12-ton, 46-foot rocket that traveled at speeds up to 4,000 mph. More than a thousand of the rockets blasted England. On the average, each V-2 caused approximately twice as many casualties as the V-1.

The flying-weapons threat did not ease until the closing months of the War, when most of the V weapons' launching sites on the Continent were captured by the Allies.

Loaded with a ton of high explosives, a V-1 is readied for its 400 mph flight to London.

A V-1 plunges earthward. Most V-1s were not seen, but when the noisy engine stopped, Londoners froze: the bomb hit several seconds later.

A few minutes before 10 p.m., some 500 four-engine bombers flew over the British units waiting to jump off and dropped 2,500 tons of bombs on the edge of the city. The bombing backfired on the Allies. Relatively few Germans were in the target area; instead, they were manning a network of elaborate fortifications that was too close to the British lines to be bombed. Most of the Germans, therefore, were unaffected by the bombing; the might of the attack fell largely on the city's population. Moreover, the bombs left such mountains of rubble and such enormous craters that later attempts to get through the town quickly and exploit its capture were frustrated.

In spite of the air and artillery preparation, the Germans fought back savagely when the attack was launched. Casualties were high on both sides. Some German strong points held out until flamethrowing tanks moved in to blast them at point-blank range.

Early on the morning of July 9, SS General Kurt Meyer, commander of the Hitler Jugend Division, after deciding to defy the standing order to "hold fast," started to evacuate his units across the Orne River. "We were meant to die in Caen," he later said, "but one just couldn't watch those youngsters being sacrificed to a senseless order." A little later, Rommel and Eberbach authorized the withdrawal. Troops of the Canadian 3rd Infantry Division completed the occupation of the Carpiquet airfield that morning at 11:15.

British and Canadian troops entered Caen early that afternoon and found the streets choked with huge blocks of stone. From the ruins came faint groans. About 6,000 men, women and children had perished; thousands more were injured. "The dead lay everywhere," recalled one witness, "not corpses, just the remains, fingers, a hand, a head, and pathetic personal belongings, a bottle of aspirin, rosary beads, torn and mud-soaked letters. . . ."

The capture of Caen cost the British about 3,500 men killed, wounded and missing, along with 80 tanks. The tanks could easily be replaced, but the infantrymen could not. Britain had been at war nearly five years now and had provided three quarters of the troops for the European campaign up to this point. Britain was running out of men. Much the same was true for the Germans, who had lost 6,000 soldiers in the Caen battle.

Bitter as it was, the battle for Caen served an invaluable purpose for the Allies. Montgomery succeeded in drawing the bulk of the German divisions into action against the British Second Army and away from the Americans to the west. It was clear from the ferocity of the German defense, however, that there was little immediate hope of cracking the enemy defenses in the Caen sector. If the stalemate in Normandy was to be broken, Bradley's First Army would have to break it.

After the fall of Cherbourg, Bradley had turned all of his forces to the south. Two critical objectives lay in the path of the American First Army. One of them was Coutances, located on the coastal road 40 miles to the south. Three major roads and two secondary routes met at Coutances; one led southward along the coast through Granville to Avranches, the gateway to Brittany and the heart of France. The First Army's other critical objective lay 15 miles to the east of Coutances at Saint-Lô, where four major roads and four secondary ones converged.

The attack to the south would lead directly through the worst of the hedgerow country, and much of the terrain over which Bradley's troops would have to move had been flooded by heavy rains in recent weeks. But Coutances seemed to be not as waterlogged as elsewhere, and Bradley placed his heavyweight VIII Corps under Major General Troy H. Middleton in that sector. The VIII Corps now contained four divisions: the 82nd Airborne, the recently transferred 79th, the 90th and the newly arrived 8th.

In the center Bradley placed Collins' VII Corps, with one untried division, the 83rd, and two seasoned ones, the 4th and the 9th. Their mission was to take the road junction of Périers and then move southeast to cut the Coutances–Saint-Lô highway.

On the left Bradley positioned the XIX Corps under the command of Major General Charles H. Corlett. Initially, the corps would have only one division, the 30th, but the 29th and the 3rd Armored would later be added. Corlett's objective was to get astride the Vire River, attack down both sides and capture Saint-Lô.

The attack began on July 3, when the men of the VIII Corps jumped off, full of confidence and optimism, believing that the Germans were worn out and would withdraw. But they encountered heavy rain and stubborn enemy resistance. Crack troops of the 82nd Airborne moved forward easily at first, then ran into fierce opposition; they ground out a total of four miles in three days at a cost of approximately 1,200 casualties.

To the east of the 82nd, the 90th and the 79th Divisions lost more than 4,000 men between them as they pushed four miles through the hedgerows. Attacking in the rain, the 90th lost over 600 men on the first day and suffered even heavier casualties the following day.

The newly committed 8th Division also had its troubles. The division was regarded as one of the best-trained outfits in the U.S. Army, but it had to learn the hard way to slip around enemy units and methodically make its way through the hedgerows.

In 12 days of fighting, the four divisions of the VIII Corps advanced seven miles at a cost of 10,000 casualties. Meanwhile, in the VII Corps sector, the 83rd Division attacked toward Périers on July 4 over soggy ground enclosed by still more hedgerows. Almost everything went wrong from the start. The attackers were plagued by deadly but invisible enemy fire. Infiltrating German infantrymen seemed to be everywhere, and the hedgerows frequently proved almost insuperable obstacles. Tanks chewed up telephone wires, commanders and their units lost communication with one another, a regimental commander was shot and snipers picked off engineers who were trying to clear minefields. By an enormous effort, the division pushed forward 200 yards, taking six prisoners and losing 47 killed, 815 wounded and 530 missing. (As if he knew how badly his opponents were faring, the commander of the German troops in the area—an elite parachute regiment—returned American medics he had captured.)

But the Germans could not be everywhere; the battle was grinding them down, too. The XIX Corps found this out on July 7, when it uncovered a weak point in the Germans' defenses. One of the 30th Division's early objectives was the little crossroad hamlet of Saint-Jean-de-Daye, straddling the north-south road to Saint-Lô. To take the village, the troops of the 30th had to cross the Vire et Taute Canal from the north and the Vire River from the east. The crossings were opposed, but resistance was so light that the commander of the corps, General Corlett, concluded that he

might make a swift stroke to the south. Bradley gave him the 3rd Armored Division, and Corlett ordered its commander, Major General Leroy H. Watson, to cross the Vire River at Airel and make a "power drive" to the south. The objective was a 300-foot hill known as Hauts-Vents, three miles down the road, dominating the Vire River bridge and the main road leading into Saint-Lô from the northwest.

The spearhead of the armored division, Combat Command B under Brigadier General John J. Bohn, had to cross the Vire at the same point where 30th Division infantrymen had already crossed. That meant putting a column more than 20 miles long, with 6,000 soldiers in 800 vehicles and trailers, across the single bridge at Airel—on a piece of ground that was already bursting with 30th Division troops and equipment, and under continuous enemy attack. All of this had to be accomplished with inexperienced troops and officers and with no time to coordinate the movements of the armored division through the territory occupied by the infantry.

Bohn's combat command was originally scheduled to follow the main road after crossing the Vire River bridge. The tanks would dash down the highway, secure the bridgehead and then turn south to provide a spearhead for a further advance. But the 3rd Armored Division's commander, General Watson, was fearful that this route would expose the tanks to flank attack by the Germans. He decided, therefore, that Bohn should turn left immediately after crossing the bridge and follow some unimproved roads and trails that would bring him out three miles below Saint-Jean-de-Daye.

This decision was to lead to an almost unbelievable succession of blunders, misfortunes and delays that would cost the luckless Bohn his future with the Army. The first thing that went wrong was that the unimproved roads and lanes proved to be so narrow that the tanks were forced to fan out over the countryside. The tanks got hopelessly bogged down among the hedgerows, and demolition teams and bulldozers had to be called up to clear a route for them through the thickets.

On the first day, Bohn's task force made only a mile and a half. Behind them eight infantry battalions, four tank battalions and three artillery battalions were jumbled together in the maze of hedgerows. In the confusion, tankers of the 3rd

The gaunt remains of the cathedral of Notre-Dame rise from the ruins of Saint-Lô, a strategic Normandy crossroads town that was almost 95 per cent destroyed before troops of the U.S. 29th Division captured it on July 18, 1944. The devastation brought about by more than a month of Allied bombing and shelling was intensified by a two-day German artillery and mortar barrage. So great was the destruction that many U.S. troops fell into an awed silence upon entering the rubble-choked streets. Said one soldier: "We sure liberated the hell out of this place."

Armored and infantrymen of the 30th Division fired at each other and 16 men were shot.

In an effort to unscramble the mess, Corlett put Major General Leland S. Hobbs, commander of the 30th Division, in charge of all the troops of the bridgehead. On July 9, Hobbs sent Bohn an ultimatum: take the objective at Hauts-Vents by 5 p.m. or be relieved. Corlett then fired off a separate message to the same effect. Bohn finally managed to get some of the tanks unsnarled and sent eight of them off in the direction of Hauts-Vents. But they were slowed by the swampy lowlands and the narrow, sunken roads and trails in the hedgerow country.

At this point, a new threat to the troops in the bridgehead suddenly loomed. Corlett and Hobbs learned from aerial reconnaissance that heavy German reinforcements, including elements of the 2nd Panzer Division and the Panzer Lehr Division, were on their way to this sector of the front. Rumors ran through the ranks, and fears mounted when a force from the 2nd SS Panzer Division struck the 30th Division near Le Désert. With strong artillery support, the 30th beat off the attack, but later a company of the 743rd Tank Battalion was ambushed by German armor with the loss of a dozen tanks and more than 40 casualties.

Reports circulated that whole battalions were being surrounded. A supply party of about 200 men on the main road south of Saint-Jean-de-Daye panicked and began running back toward the intersection in small groups.

In the meantime, Bohn's missing eight tanks started down a narrow lane and got lost among the hedgerows. When the tanks finally emerged on the main road to Saint-Jean-de-Daye, instead of turning left, as they were supposed to, they turned right.

This proved to be a fatal mistake. It brought them directly into range of the 823rd Tank Destroyer Battalion, an American outfit that had deployed its guns on both sides of the main road to protect Saint-Jean-de-Daye from the south.

The tank-destroyer gunners were edgy because they had been getting reports that German tanks were in the area. When the silhouette of a tank appeared at the top of a rise 3,000 yards away, they thought it was German. But they double-checked by radio to headquarters to ask whether any American armor was in the area. The answer was no—any tanks in the vicinity must belong to the enemy. By now several tanks had come into view, turrets rotating as they fired machine-gun bullets and occasional high-explosive shells into the hedges and fields bordering the road.

The first round from the tank destroyers, fired at a range of 600 yards, slammed into the lead tank and wounded the commander. At that moment Bohn, who was trying to get in touch with the eight tanks on the open radio channel, clearly heard the stricken tank commander say, "I am in dreadful agony."

The lead tank and one other were knocked out, and in the exchange of gunfire, 10 tank and tank-destroyer crewmen were wounded. The six remaining tanks quickly turned around and headed south toward Hauts-Vents.

At this point, Hobbs decided that the tanks were getting overextended. He sent an order to Bohn to halt the tanks where they were and have them button up for the night. Bohn tried to reach the six tanks by radio but was unable to get through to them.

The little advance force went rumbling down the road to Hauts-Vents and arrived there shortly after dark. They were just in time to be strafed by U.S. planes, which were supposed to have attacked Hauts-Vents much earlier but had been delayed by bad weather.

By now Bohn had suffered through an almost incredible series of frustrations and snafus. His orders had been switched before his tanks crossed the bridge, and as a result the armor had become entangled with the infantrymen of the 30th Division. The eight tanks that had finally managed to unscramble themselves had become lost, had taken the wrong road and had been shot up by their own side.

That night Hobbs relieved Bohn of his command. "I know what you did personally," Hobbs said, "but you are a victim of circumstance."

The fired general was understandably bitter. Hobbs had ordered him to take Hauts-Vents or be removed, then had told him to call off the tank attack on that objective. Bohn had tried his best to reach the tanks, but had been prevented because their radios were out of order. The tanks had proceeded to take the objective, only to be strafed by American planes. "You spend your whole life preparing for combat," Bohn said, "and the whole thing goes down the drain in three days."

Bohn may have been well out of it. However, the worst was still to come.

The Panzer Lehr Division attempted to launch a counterattack in the early hours of July 11, but the effort merely proved that the hedgerow country was no better place for German tanks than it was for Allied tanks. The German division managed to penetrate U.S. positions in two areas, but troops of the combat-wise 9th Infantry Division, which had fought in Tunisia and Sicily, worked their way around through the hedgerows and closed in behind the attacking enemy tanks. The infantrymen then sealed off the Germans' escape routes, and American tanks, tank destroyers and bazookas mauled the enemy armor. Heavy casualties were inflicted; one unit that had started the counterattack with six officers, 40 noncoms, 198 men and 10 tanks was reduced to seven noncoms and 23 men—without tanks or officers.

With the German counterattack stalled, the American XIX Corps resumed its advance, but exhaustion forced it to stop near the Lessay–Périers–Saint-Lô highway. In the meantime, farther west, the VIII Corps, after battling its way through seven miles of hedgerows, also halted within sight of that road. At this point, Coutances, only 14 miles ahead, seemed as unreachable as Berlin. The VII Corps, sloshing around in the muck south of Carentan, was forced to stop four miles short of Périers.

The fighting among the hedgerows had now proved to be

so costly that Bradley's original objective—the Coutances–Saint-Lô highway—seemed unattainable. Just to reach the line from Lessay to Caumont, the First Army had suffered 40,000 casualties, 90 per cent of them infantrymen. Bradley knew that the American offensive was bogged down badly. He needed to do something decisive soon. By now most of the attacking units of the First Army had arrived at the Lessay–Périers–Saint-Lô road. That road was only partway out of the murderous hedgerow country that the men had been fighting through for the last couple of weeks, but it would have to do as the platform for the next offensive.

That offensive was already taking form in Bradley's mind. But before he could do anything else he had to capture the road junction at Saint-Lô and secure his flank on the left.

Once charming and serene, Saint-Lô had been a favorite leave spot for the German occupiers before June 6, but Allied bombing had turned it into a pile of rubble, and 800 civilians lay dead in the ruins.

The assignment of capturing Saint-Lô fell to the 29th Division. The Germans held out stubbornly on Martinville Ridge, east of the town, until the 2nd Battalion of the 116th Regiment, under Major Sidney V. Bingham, found a weak spot and advanced to within 1,000 yards of Saint-Lô. Bingham's battalion was cut off, but he reported by radio that he thought he could hold out.

Early the next morning, the 3rd Battalion, under Major Thomas D. Howie, moved out under cover of heavy mist to relieve Bingham's isolated group. Combat-wise Germans, knowing that the mist could conceal just such a movement, stepped up their artillery fire and poured machine-gun bullets into the murk. Howie's men crept forward and held their own fire. After several hours they worked their way through to Bingham's men. Both units were then supposed to move on and enter the outskirts of Saint-Lô, but Bingham's battalion was no longer fit to make the effort. On the radio the commander of the 29th Division, Major General Charles H. Gerhardt, asked Howie if he could move his battalion to the edge of town all by itself. Howie replied "Will do." Moments later he was killed by a shellburst.

Both battalions were now cut off, mainly by German shellfire. Efforts to break through to them with food, ammunition and medical supplies failed. A column of half-tracks and tank destroyers tried to negotiate sunken roads that were clogged with wrecked vehicles and dead German transport horses, but progress under the German barrage was impossible.

On the night of July 17, riflemen of the 116th Infantry Regiment finally broke through to the two isolated battalions. The following morning the final assault on Saint-Lô was launched. A task force under the command of Brigadier General Norman D. Cota, the assistant division commander, picked its way through antitank artillery and mortar fire to a square close to the town's cemetery. Using the square as a base of operations, infantry, tanks and tank destroyers then moved forward to seize key points in the town. By 5 p.m., after a series of skirmishes, Saint-Lô was in American hands. As the troops pushed into the center of town, the body of Major Howie was draped with an American flag, taken aboard a jeep and transported to the center of Saint-Lô. There it was gently laid on a pile of rubble before the old Romanesque church of Sainte Croix to serve as a symbol of the casualties suffered at Saint-Lô. All around it lay the ruins of the devastated town.

The Germans attempted a counterattack that night, but their forces were so badly weakened that it failed.

Saint-Lô, like Caen, had finally fallen, and the Allies were at last emerging from the sodden hedgerow country onto firm, dry ground. But all of this had come at a tremendous cost. The British, Americans and Canadians had suffered 122,000 casualties since the Normandy landings. The Allies had inflicted tremendous losses on the enemy—over 115,000 men were killed, wounded or missing—but they still had not been able to smash through the German defenses and get on with the liberation of the rest of France. Before that could be accomplished, another massive attack would be required.

SHAMBLES AT CHERBOURG

From atop newly won Fort du Roule, U.S. VII Corps commander Major General J. Lawton Collins views smoking Cherbourg harbor facilities set afire by Germans.

CLEARING A PASSAGE INTO A VITAL HARBOR

When, after more than a week of battle, the U.S. VII Corps won the badly needed port of Cherbourg at the end of June 1944, it seemed to Allied engineers that the harbor could be cleared in three weeks. Reconstruction plans that had been drawn up more than a year in advance had taken into account German sabotage, and special teams of divers had undergone extensive training in the muddy waters of England's Thames River, learning how to search out and defuse mines.

But when the damage was surveyed, it proved much more extensive than anyone had foreseen. The Germans had left basins and docks blocked by more than 55 scuttled ships, barges and smaller craft, and by overturned cranes and dynamited bridges. They had also wrecked docking and unloading facilities, including piers, wharves, storehouses, railways and utilities, in addition to 95 per cent of the crucial deepwater quay area that was needed by the Allies for their supply ships.

Hundreds of mines hampered clearing operations. Not satisfied with wrecking a railway bridge, the Germans had mined the sections of it that remained above water. And to confuse the Allies, they had marked minefields where there were none—and then booby-trapped the signs. The problem was worse in the water. No one could tell where or when a mine might go off—or what might trigger it. Some mines were so sensitive to changes in the magnetic field that the mere presence of a ship 125 feet above was enough to detonate them. During the course of the work, more than 200 mines went off, sinking three minesweepers and seven other craft and damaging three more.

In spite of the dangers, the clearing operations proceeded at fever pitch. By the 16th of July—three weeks after the capture of Cherbourg—four Liberty ships unloaded the first supplies in the harbor. But many more weeks would be required before the port could begin to meet the quota of 8,000 tons of cargo per day set for it by the planners—10 times the peacetime amount.

The first U.S. Naval Salvage unit rolls up to a statue of Napoleon at Cherbourg harbor on July 6, 1944. The statue overlooked the Avant Port du Commerce, a valuable anchorage that had been so thoroughly blocked and mined by the Germans that it took five weeks to clear it.

The remains of a bridge and a scuttled barge awash in a sea of debris block an entrance to the deepwater Avant Port du Commerce, which was needed by Liberty ships at Cherbourg. Seven more vessels—one of them heavily mined—and a 100-ton floating crane clogged the basin itself.

Readying Cherbourg to receive ships, the U.S.S. Pinon reels in torn German torpedo nets and their buoys to replace them with new nets and buoys spanning the harbor mouth.

BOOBY TRAPS AND BLOCKED BOAT BASINS

Clearing Cherbourg harbor of all of the wreckage and mines left behind by the Germans required great resourcefulness.

While engineers built docks and blasted holes in the sea wall to facilitate immediate unloading onto the shore, salvage units labored in the murky water. Sunken vessels were patched at low tide and pumped free of water so they could be floated away at high tide; vessels too badly damaged to patch were raised by pontoons strapped to them when the tide ran out. A sunken submarine-lifting vessel had to be blasted into manageable pieces by explosives, and

toppled cranes were cut into sections by divers using acetylene torches.

Removing mines proved a nightmarish task. Minesweepers had to contend with not only three types of mines commonly used by the Germans—those detonated by magnetic, acoustic or direct contact with a ship—but also a fourth kind the Allies dubbed "Katies." These concrete-encased contraptions rested on the floor of the harbor two to three fathoms down, well out of the reach of ordinary minesweepers, and exploded as ships passed overhead. Some Katies had been set to go off only after several ships had sailed over them. Other mines had delayed-action fuses that detonated up to 85 days after being set.

To locate mines and obstacles, divers,

hooked up by telephone to launches that followed on the surface, spent six weeks scouring the entire harbor floor. The divers walked along lines sunk to guide them through the darkness. When they found a mine, they identified it by touch and then dismantled it if they could, or had it raised to the surface where sharpshooters waited to explode it.

Clearing mines seemed a never-ending task—a single barge sunk by the Germans concealed more than 65 mines of differing varieties, which took divers three weeks to remove. Two weeks of intensive minesweeping were required to open a narrow passage for ships, and three and a half months were needed before the harbor could be considered safe.

A geyser erupts outside the breakwaters of Cherbourg harbor as two British minesweepers detonate an underwater mine in July 1944. Sixteen sweeps were made every morning to set off delayed-action mines.

The tension of his task evident in his face, a member of the U.S. Navy Salvage team uses a hacksaw to cut a bundle of electrical cables laid by the Germans to trigger the mines they had hidden in Cherbourg.

A member of a bomb disposal squad saws through the detonating cap of a delayed-action mine discovered in a Cherbourg cellar. Attached to a pipe, the mine had been set to spray noxious chemicals into the street.

British sailors help members of a specially trained team put on diving suits used when scouring Cherbourg harbor for mines.

A U.S. Navy Salvage ship moors alongside an overturned 550-foot-long whaler that was later used to extend a rebuilt pier.

A floating crane swings over the wreckage of a 1,700-ton submarine-lifting vessel blocking a harbor basin. The vessel's bridge had already been removed.

Smoke billows up from a sea wall at Cherbourg harbor as U.S. Army engineers use dynamite to open one of three breaches that allowed unloading on the beach.

U.S. troops begin breaking up concrete rubble with jackhammers to clear a dock in Cherbourg harbor.

Derricks used for unloading cargo line a 4,200-foot wooden pier being built up and out from a sea wall.

With no deep-draft berths yet available, the first Liberty ship to enter Cherbourg harbor had to have its cargo unloaded and ferried to the shore by an LCT.

THE TRICKY TASK OF UNLOADING SUPPLIES

The Allies needed supplies so badly that they could not afford to wait while Cherbourg harbor was cleared of all mines, obstacles and rubble. As soon as a channel was opened through the harbor in mid-July, ships began unloading cargo. LCTs and DUK-Ws ferried supplies from the vessels to the beach front.

But even when overloaded by 100 per cent, as was frequently the case, the amphibian lighters could manage only a few thousand tons of supplies a day, far short of Allied needs. Creating deepwater berths for ships for direct unloading was vital.

Working both night and day, engineers cleared and repaired a severely damaged breakwater, the Digue du Homet, in four days. Then they built five wooden piers along the breakwater and filled the gaps to form a continuous quay 2,700 feet long. Next they laid railroad tracks to provide access to train ferries. On August 9 the first Liberty ship docked alongside the quay.

By November, Cherbourg was handling more than 14,000 tons of supplies a day—6,000 tons more than the goal set for it. Against all odds, the harbor had become the most important port in the continental supply network, responsible for half the supplies brought in by American forces.

The harbor's first Liberty ship lowers a net containing Signal Corps wire spools to a waiting DUK-W.

Laden with cargo, a DUK-W plows through swells on its way to the beach-front unloading area.

A British train ferry and two Liberty ships unload their cargo at the rebuilt Digue du Homet breakwater in August 1944. By the end of the month, Cherbourg harbor had handled almost 300,000 tons of essential supplies.

Traffic backs up at the beach front as newly arrived two-and-a-half-ton trucks wait for incoming freight. DUK-Ws lined up in the second and third rows were to pick up supplies from ships anchored in the outer harbor.

A scant month after salvage operations got under way, a locomotive is hoisted ashore from the seatrain Texas by the booms of a crane ship moored alongside. Lighter railroad cars were rolled directly onto tracks.

2

BREAKOUT

While American troops were still struggling through the hedgerows north of Saint-Lô, General Bradley, commander of the U.S. First Army, gave his aide, Major Chester B. Hansen, a top-priority order. Hansen was to locate a large mess tent and have it set up adjacent to the general's command-post truck. The tent must have a wooden floor, and Hansen was to install in it the largest map of the Normandy beachhead that he could find.

By now Bradley was fed up with the agonizing and extremely costly progress of the hedgerow fighting. He had been ordered by General Montgomery to find a way to break out of the beachhead, and he intended to study the map until he came up with a solution. For that purpose he needed a map that would show in detail every road and terrain feature of the beachhead area. He also needed a floor, because heavy rains had recently turned the Normandy countryside into a sea of mud and he expected to do a lot of pacing before the map.

When Hansen took his problem to the headquarters commandant—the officer in charge of housekeeping around the command post—he met with some resistance at first. "Now you're pampering the old man," the headquarters commandant said. "Who ever heard of a wooden floor in a tent in the field?"

But with the authority of a three-star general behind him, Hansen got what he wanted. A floor was constructed of planks, the tent was set up, and an enormous eight-foot map of the Normandy beachhead was installed.

Bradley spent the next two nights in the tent studying the map, sketching in division and corps boundaries with colored pencils and marking roads and rivers. As he paced back and forth, he devised a plan. First Army troops would attack the enemy along a narrow front—but not until after Allied heavy bombers had pounded the Germans so hard that they would be unable to fight back when the ground assault got under way.

Ground and air efforts would have to be coordinated with great precision. To gain the maximum advantage from the bombing, the infantry would have to be as close as possible to the target area, ready to move as soon as the planes completed their runs. As Bradley studied the map, his attention fastened on the old road running east-west from Saint-Lô to Périers. Built by the Romans, the road was ruler-straight; it could serve as a marker that would clearly set off the Americans from the Germans on the other side of it, a marker that would be readily recognizable from the air. First Army troops were now approaching this road, and with some luck they would soon be in position to push across it for an attack to the south.

Using a colored pencil, Bradley drew a rectangle on the map, covering an area three and a half miles wide and a mile and a half deep, south of the Périers–Saint-Lô road. This would be the critical area of battle; the bombers would fly in parallel to the road and carpet-bomb the rectangle. Then, upon completion of the bombing, two infantry divisions would assault enemy positions, tear open a large gap and hold back the sides for a motorized infantry division to come through. The motorized division would dash all the way to Coutances, 15 miles to the southwest. Two armored divisions would then follow. While one provided protection against German attacks on the flank to the east, the other would go barreling down to Avranches—a distance of 30 miles—and turn the corner into Brittany.

This was the plan for what came to be known as the Normandy breakout. Given the code name *Cobra,* the operation would later be fairly described by Bradley as "the most decisive battle of our war in western Europe."

On July 10, two days after Bradley first hatched his plan, General Montgomery called a conference at his headquarters at Creuilly with Bradley and General Dempsey of the British Second Army, his two top subordinates. In the course of the meeting, Bradley informed Montgomery of his plan for the breakout. He explained that the attack could not get started until his dwindling supplies of ammunition had been replenished and First Army troops were within hailing distance of the Périers–Saint-Lô road.

Understanding Bradley's need for time, Montgomery decided to do whatever he could to enlarge the scope of the offensive and ensure its success. He ordered Dempsey to make a "massive stroke" in the Caen-Falaise area. Three armored divisions of the British VIII Corps—the 7th, the 11th and the Guards—would be set aside for the attack. The armored divisions would be supported by the Canadian II Corps and the British XII Corps. Thus, instead of being struck by *Cobra* alone, the Germans now would receive a double blow. The new operation was code-named *Goodwood,* and planning for it began.

On July 13, three days after meeting with Bradley and Dempsey, Montgomery sent a message to General Eisenhower that said, "Am going to launch a very big attack next week." He explained that the British Second Army would push forward in the area south of Caen and the U.S. First Army would follow up with an assault west of Saint-Lô. Montgomery took pains to point out that the success of the operation would depend to a large extent upon having "the whole weight" of Allied air power behind it. If all went well, he said, *Goodwood* might have "far-reaching results."

Eisenhower took this to mean that Montgomery intended a breakout in the Caen area—an assumption that was to lead to misunderstandings later. "With respect to the plan," he wrote, "I am confident that it will reap a harvest from all the sowing that you have been doing during the past weeks. . . . I am not discounting the difficulties, nor the initial losses, but in this case I am viewing the prospects with the most tremendous optimism and enthusiasm. I would not be at all surprised to see you gaining a victory that will make some of the old classics look like a skirmish between patrols." Ike assured Montgomery that he could count on Bradley "to keep his troops fighting like the very devil, twenty-four hours a day, to provide the opportunity your armored corps will need, and to make the victory complete."

On July 14 one of Montgomery's aides, Lieut. Colonel Christopher Dawnay, arrived in London to brief the War Office on *Goodwood.* He stated that its "real object is to muck up and write off the enemy troops" and indicated that Montgomery "has no intention of rushing madly eastward and getting Second Army so extended that the flank might cease to be secure." He did add, however, that Montgomery stood "ready to take advantage of any situation which gives reason to think that the enemy is disintegrating." Despite Dawnay's assurances to the contrary, Allied air commanders were sure from the magnitude of the air support requested that Montgomery intended to achieve a breakout. An aerial bombardment of such scope surely would not be needed just to tie down German troops.

Goodwood was set for July 17, *Cobra* for the 18th. Air Chief Marshal Sir Arthur Tedder gave Montgomery his assurance that he would arrange for the heavy air support required by "the far-reaching and decisive plan." What Tedder arranged, in fact, was a stupendous show—the largest number of planes yet brought together in support of a ground attack. All told, some 1,600 British and American heavy bombers, plus another 400 medium bombers and fighter-bombers, were called for. These were to drop a total of 7,800 tons of bombs on German defenses; 2,500 tons were earmarked for the industrial suburbs of Caen, where the Germans were holed up, another 650 tons for the fortified village of Cagny just south of Caen and still more for other enemy positions in the target area.

Special care was taken to coordinate the air and ground attacks and to avoid a costly interval that would give the Germans time to recover. The bombers must not be allowed to crater the roads that the armored units would use in their drive forward. The planes were to use 260-pound fragmentation bombs to avoid this. As soon as the saturation bombing was completed, the armored divisions of O'Connor's VIII Corps, supported by 720 artillery pieces, would dash across two railroad embankments and seize the Bourguébus ridge, a commanding feature of the Falaise plain. The plain offered splendid tank country, and the main road beyond the ridge ran straight to Falaise, 15 miles to the south.

Thanks to the commander of Army Group B, Field Marshal Rommel, the Germans were prepared for the Goodwood offensive. Rommel had deployed his forces in depth to prevent a breakthrough. Facing the British along a 70-mile front was General Eberbach's Panzer Group West, consisting of four corps made up of eight divisions in the line and five divisions in reserve. Eberbach's battle positions were organized into five defensive zones: first the deeply entrenched infantry, then the tanks, next a band of fortified villages, then 88mm guns, artillery and rocket launchers emplaced on the Bourguébus ridge, and finally, reserve divisions positioned approximately five miles to the rear.

To make sure everything was in readiness, Rommel made a final inspection of these defenses on the afternoon of July 17. On his way back to his headquarters, his car was spotted by British planes. Rommel called out to his driver to take cover, but the fighters swooped in so quickly that the driver was killed at the wheel. The automobile swerved into a tree, and Rommel was thrown to the road. Suffering from concussion, he was carried unconscious to a village that by one of the War's strange ironies was called Sainte-Foy-de-Montgommery. He survived the accident and was sent home to Germany to recuperate, but his illustrious military career was at an end.

The German dispositions that Rommel had so carefully nurtured were suddenly weakened on the eve of Goodwood, when Hitler became convinced that an Allied landing near the mouth of the Seine was imminent. The Führer ordered Field Marshal von Kluge, who had replaced Rommel as commander of Army Group B, to send a panzer division from the Caen area to Lisieux, not far from the river's mouth. Kluge protested to OKW, the German High Command, citing the dangers on the Caen front. "We aren't strong enough there," he said. He preferred to take his chances on another landing and to keep the panzer division where it was.

"I'll transmit your opinion to the Führer," the staff officer at OKW said.

"Never mind," Kluge said quickly. "You don't have to tell him anything more. I just wanted to talk it over with you."

The Goodwood air bombardment got under way at 5:30 on the morning of July 18. RAF Pathfinders dropped flares, and then 1,000 Lancasters and Halifaxes let loose a torrent of bombs. An infantryman, who watched while waiting for his outfit to move out, later wrote down his impressions: "The bombers flew in majestically and with a dreadful, unalterable dignity, unloaded and made for home; the sun, just coming over the horizon, caught their wings as they wheeled. Now hundreds of little black clouds were puffing round the bombers as they droned inexorably to their targets and occasionally one of them would heel over and plunge smoothly into the huge pall of smoke and dust that was steadily growing in the south. Everyone was out of their vehicles now, staring in awed wonder till the last wave dropped its bombs and turned away."

The RAF bombing lasted 45 minutes. When it was over, the unnerved German survivors climbed from their shelters to find villages and farmhouses around them obliterated. In minutes they had to dash for cover again as 571 American Eighth Air Force heavy bombers came over and pounded the area. Though the bombardiers found it difficult to sight bombs accurately through the smoke and dust raised by the earlier bombing, they nevertheless managed to eliminate many of the assault guns and panzer grenadiers at Démouville. Despite the intensity of the British and American bombing, the backbone of General Eberbach's defense system, the 88mm guns on the Bourguébus ridge, escaped serious damage.

Following the bombing, Canadian troops attacked the industrial suburbs of Caen across the Orne River from the city. In spite of the careful advance planning for the raid, bomb craters in the roads slowed the Canadians and gave the Germans time to recover from the bombing and stiffen their defenses. It took the Canadians the rest of the day and well into the night to clear the industrial area. At the same time, the British tanks moved out on schedule, 32 in a wave. The tanks lost formation as they entered the dust and smoke

raised by the bombs, but they encountered little opposition where the bombs had fallen. Dazed German infantrymen staggered toward them to surrender; others were too stunned even to rise from their foxholes.

Bomb craters in the paths of the tanks forced some of them to detour and slowed their progress. And in areas where bombs had not fallen, the Germans fought back hard, and many of the tanks were hit. "I watched through the periscope, fascinated, as though it was a film I was seeing," Lance Corporal Ron Cox later remembered. "Then suddenly there was a tremendous crash and shudder. We had been hit. It was a glancing blow but the track was broken. The next shot would follow as soon as the enemy gun could be reloaded. Wally Herd shouted, 'Bail out!' As we bailed out and ran, crouched down away from the tank, it was hit a second time and smoke began to pour from it."

For all the difficulties, the VIII Corps advanced more than

Taking cover behind cow carcasses, two American infantrymen advance under heavy fire along the Carentan-Périers road on July 22, 1944. "We must have seen a thousand dead cows in Normandy, perhaps two thousand," wrote one Allied observer. "One could never get used to that appalling sweet sickly stench." Most of the livestock was killed by Allied saturation bombing and the artillery shelling of both sides.

35 aircraft in the second formation dropped theirs—after making three runs to identify the target. But more than 300 bombers in the third formation dropped 550 tons of high explosives and 135 tons of fragmentation bombs before turning back.

Some of the bombs fell on American ground positions and killed 25 men, wounded another 131 and left some units in such shock that the men were unable to stir.

Bradley was horrified. He had expected the bombers to make a lateral approach, along the road, but the planes had come in over the heads of his troops. He protested to Leigh-Mallory, saying that he had left the July 19 meeting with "a clear understanding they would fly parallel to that road." Leigh-Mallory replied that he had been forced to leave the conference before that part of the discussion, but he promised to check into the matter and call Bradley back.

The size of the bombs used also disturbed Bradley. He had expected 100-pound fragmentation bombs—but the ones dropped had all been bigger and more powerful.

The abortive bombing had sown confusion up and down the line. Word that Leigh-Mallory had called off the bombardment had reached General Collins, the commander of the attacking American VII Corps, shortly before the bombs began landing. Collins did not know whether *Cobra* had been delayed or was proceeding according to plan after all.

As he ordered his troops to the jump-off point, he was surprised to discover that the enemy had moved into the area earlier vacated by the Americans. Two infantry divisions now had to struggle to take back the ground that had been given up for their own safety. One battalion gained a single hedgerow; two other battalions fought eight hours to reduce a strong point. Enemy artillery fire was heavy, and all advancing units took heavy casualties.

Across the Périers–Saint-Lô road, the German Panzer Lehr Division waited. The division commander, Major General Fritz Bayerlein, was sure that the bombing signaled the beginning of a major attack. Yet his communications were so badly mangled that he found it extremely difficult to coordinate a defensive effort. When the Americans failed to push across the road, he congratulated his troops for turning back a major attack. His losses were relatively light, his front line was intact, and he had committed no reserves. Then he made a fateful decision: he moved more troops

into the rectangular target area, unaware that the saturation bombing had been rescheduled for 11 o'clock the following morning, July 25.

The raid had been carefully worked out by the ground and air commanders. More than 1,500 B-17s and B-24s would fly over the target area and drop 3,300 tons of bombs; 400 medium bombers would release another 650 tons, and 550 fighter-bombers would drop more than 200 tons of high explosives and napalm. The bombardment was to be intensified by 125,000 rounds fired by artillery. To prevent a recurrence of the tragedy of the day before, the bombardiers were ordered not to release bombs above the Périers–Saint-Lô road. A special weather plane was to check visibility in the early morning. If the weather was good, the heavy bombers would fly in as low as possible and the bombardiers would sight the targets visually instead of using instruments.

Before the attack got under way, Bradley received the promised telephone call from Leigh-Mallory, who said that he had checked with the Air Force and found the overhead approach to the target area had not been a mistake. The air planners were opposed to a lateral run because it would mean approaching and entering the rectangular target area through its narrow side. The planes not only would have to fly dangerously close together but also would be exposed for a longer period of time to German antiaircraft guns, deployed across the entire length of the rectangle. If Bradley wanted the air bombardment resumed, Leigh-Mallory made it clear that the First Army commander would have to agree to let the planes come in over the heads of the troops. Bradley was angry at what he considered a breach of faith by the Air Force, but he acquiesced because he could see no alternative.

Americans on the ground were elated when they caught sight of the majestic armada. Correspondent Ernie Pyle, who had joined the men of the 4th Division for the *Cobra* operation, stood out in the open with them, transfixed by the sight of the oncoming planes.

"We spread our feet and leaned far back trying to look straight up, until our steel helmets fell off," he wrote. "And then the bombs came. They began like the crackle of popcorn and almost instantly swelled into a monstrous fury of noise that seemed surely to destroy all the world ahead of us." A wall of dust and smoke rose into the sky and "sifted around us and into our noses. The bright day grew slowly dark from it." And all the while the noise grew, becoming "an indescribable caldron of sounds."

As Pyle and the GIs watched, "there crept into our consciousness a realization that the windrows of exploding bombs were easing back toward us, flight by flight, instead of gradually forward, as the plan called for. Then we were horrified by the suspicion that those machines, high in the sky and completely detached from us, were aiming their bombs at the smoke line on the ground—and a gentle breeze was drifting the smoke line back over us! An inde-

scribable kind of panic came over us. We stood tensed in muscle and frozen in intellect, watching each flight approach and pass over, feeling trapped and completely helpless. And then all of an instant the universe became filled with a gigantic rattling as of huge ripe seeds in a mammoth dry gourd. I doubt that any of us had ever heard that sound before, but instinct told us what it was. It was bombs by the hundred, hurtling down through the air above us.

"Many times I've heard bombs whistle or swish or rustle, but never before had I heard bombs rattle. I still don't know the explanation of it. But it is an awful sound. We dived. Some got into a dugout. Others made foxholes and ditches and some got behind a garden wall. I was too late for the

Closely guarded by a Canadian soldier, a despondent German officer sits with his head in his hands after being captured south of Caen during the Goodwood operation. Between D-Day and the 25th of July, the Canadian and British troops took approximately 11,500 Germans prisoner.

dugout. The nearest place was a wagon shed. The rattle was right down upon us. I remember hitting the ground flat, all spread out like the cartoons of people flattened by steam rollers, and then squirming like an eel to get under one of the heavy wagons in the shed.

"An officer whom I didn't know was wriggling beside me. The bombs were already crashing around us. We lay with our heads slightly up—like two snakes—staring at each other . . . in a futile appeal, our faces about a foot apart, until it was over."

For the second time in two days bombs had fallen on Americans. Bomb loads from 35 heavy bombers and 42 medium bombers exploded inside the American lines. One hundred eleven men were killed and 490 wounded. Among the victims was Lieut. General Lesley J. McNair, a senior member of the U.S. Army staff in Washington, who had joined a frontline battalion as an observer. Infantry command posts, an artillery-fire-direction center and vehicles were wrecked, communications were disrupted, and troops were buried in their foxholes.

Many men who were unharmed physically suffered concussion and shock. "A lot of the men were sitting around after the bombing in a complete daze," wrote a company

commander. "I called battalion and told them I was in no condition to move, that everything was completely disorganized and it would take me some time to get my men back together, and asked for a delay. But battalion said no, push off. Jump off immediately."

As word of the casualties reached higher headquarters, resentment mounted. Eisenhower was so upset that he decided he would never again use heavy bombers in support of a ground attack.

In spite of the tragic losses, the bombing had achieved its intended effect. Across the Périers–Saint-Lô road, 1,000 men of the Panzer Lehr Division had perished, and the survivors were stunned. The division commander, General Bayerlein, later reported, "my front lines looked like the face of the moon, and at least 70 per cent of my troops were out of action—dead, wounded, crazed or numbed. All my forward tanks were knocked out, and the roads were practically impassable."

Some of the survivors would be deaf for 24 hours. Three battalion command posts simply vanished, along with a whole parachute regiment. Only a dozen tanks remained operable. As Bayerlein frantically tried to restore a semblance of order by calling up units from the rear, American

P-38s, P-47s and P-51s and British Typhoons continued to blast his troops and tanks.

Now the ground attack got under way. Three American infantry divisions moved forward. General Collins intended them to take the towns of Marigny and Saint-Gilles by the end of the day so that he could send his motorized infantry and armor roaring down through the gap. But progress was slowed by the hedgerows, and by nightfall neither Marigny nor Saint-Gilles had fallen. The next day, Collins nevertheless sent his armor rolling through the infantry. One column was ordered to seize Marigny and turn southwest for Coutances, while the second column was to enter Saint-Gilles and block any effort the Germans might make to interfere with the drive to Coutances.

Saint-Gilles fell to the 2nd Armored Division in the afternoon, but infantrymen of the motorized 1st Division—who had been charged with freeing the road—could not clear the Germans from the high ground around Marigny that day. The town finally fell the third morning, and the way was open for the thrust to Coutances.

The situation was fluid now, but still fraught with danger. German troops, tanks and antitank guns lay concealed behind the hedgerows; they frequently closed in behind American mobile units and cut them off from the rear.

Bomb craters, wrecked vehicles and traffic congestion hindered the advance. But by evening Bradley knew that *Cobra* was achieving its purpose. "Things on our front really look good," he told Eisenhower. Instead of halting to consolidate his gains, he decided to go all out to smash the Germans, who by now were so demoralized that they were incapable of organizing a coordinated defense.

Seeing the enemy in flight in "bits and pieces," Bradley figured that the Germans' only hope was to regroup behind the Sée River at Avranches. Even there they could hardly make a stand unless fresh troops were brought up—and no such troops were available.

Meanwhile, Lieut. General George S. Patton Jr. had been waiting impatiently in an apple orchard on the Cotentin Peninsula for his Third Army to swing into action. But since the Third Army was not due to become operational until August 1, Bradley ordered Patton to see to it that the VIII Corps got to Avranches in a hurry.

Patton put two armored divisions at the head of the VIII Corps' advance, and late on July 28, Coutances fell to his armored thrust. The units hardly had time to savor their

U.S. troops dig out comrades who were buried when Allied bombs fell short of target during the July 25 air strike that preceded the Cobra breakout operation in Normandy. The bombings produced some 600 American casualties.

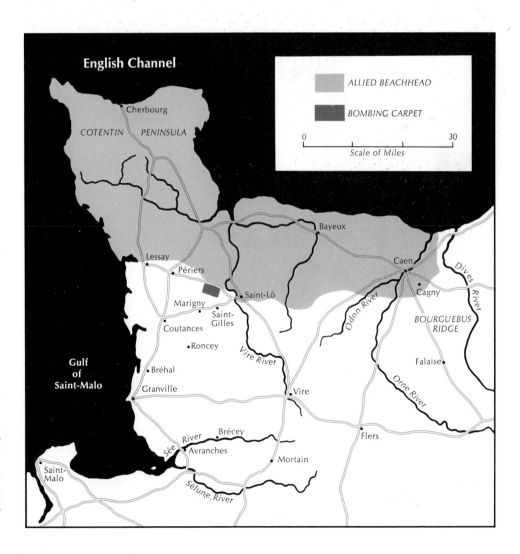

By the third week in July 1944, the Allies controlled a large part of Normandy, including all of the Cotentin Peninsula, and were ready to break out of their beachhead. For the offensive, Lieut. General Omar N. Bradley devised a plan whereby Allied planes would "carpet bomb" a rectangle measuring three and a half by one and a half miles (shown in red) south of the Périers–Saint-Lô road. The bombing was designed to tear a hole in the German lines through which the U.S. First Army could plunge south toward Coutances and Avranches and achieve the crucial breakout.

victory; by now they had their eyes set on Avranches, 30 miles farther down the road.

The Germans were in full retreat. Vehicular columns fled pell-mell to the south. Burning vehicles and tanks lined almost every road; unused mines lay scattered alongside the highways and in the haste of withdrawal, the German troops neglected to set off bridge demolitions.

Near Roncey, a huge German force had become bottled up trying to escape down the Cotentin Peninsula, and Allied aircraft discovered the traffic jam—at least 500 enemy vehi-

cles stalled bumper to bumper around the town. On the afternoon of July 29, squadrons of fighter-bombers attacked for six hours, and American artillery, tanks and tank destroyers joined in. At the end of the attack more than 100 tanks and 250 vehicles lay wrecked or abandoned.

The speed of the Americans' advance actually spread confusion through their own ranks, for, while racing around the countryside, units were getting out of touch and running into one another. In order to keep the momentum going, generals directed traffic at the critical intersections.

Pockmarked with hundreds of craters, the countryside near Saint-Lô bears the scars of saturation bombing for Operation Cobra, the breakout from the Normandy beachhead. On July 25, 1944, some 2,500 Allied planes dropped 4,000 tons of high explosives and bombs on a rectangular area of five and a quarter square miles where the German forces were massed.

Along the West coast of the Cotentin Peninsula, the advance was even more hectic. The two armored divisions leading the VIII Corps were roaring down the road to Avranches. So many enemy soldiers were surrendering that frontline units could not handle them all. "Send them to the rear disarmed without guards" became the order of the day.

Outside Bréhal, 16 miles north of Avranches, the Germans had blocked the road with heavy logs. Four P-47s were called in and tried to blast an opening in the roadblock, but not until the lead tank charged into the barrier and broke through could the American armored column resume its drive to Avranches. As the column closed in on the German Seventh Army command post, three and a half miles north of the town, General Hausser and his staff officers managed to make a hairbreadth escape through a gap between the onrushing vehicles.

Just before nightfall on July 30, troops of the 4th Armored Division crossed the undefended highway bridges over the Sée River and entered Avranches. Behind them a large German vehicular column came rolling down the coastal road from Granville. The vehicles bore red crosses, and the Americans assumed that they carried German wounded. The first few trucks were allowed to cross the bridge into town. Then the German soldiers inside the trucks opened fire. An American tank knocked out the lead vehicles, bringing the column to a halt. The Germans piled out and came toward the bridge with their hands raised in surrender. When the vehicles were inspected, they were found to be loaded with ammunition.

Now a second and larger German column came down the road to Avranches and lobbed a shell into the Americans at the bridge, striking an ammunition truck and setting it on fire. The Americans withdrew, abandoning the bridge and several hundred prisoners. The German column then crossed the bridge; some of the vehicles turned eastward to escape toward Mortain, others bumped into Americans and confused fighting took place.

For the Germans the situation had become, as Kluge called it, a "Riesensauerei"—roughly, one hell of a mess. "It's a madhouse here," he reported over the telephone on the morning of July 31 as he tried to describe what was happening. "You can't imagine what it's like. Commanders are completely out of contact."

Kluge was told that higher headquarters wanted to know whether he was setting up defenses somewhere in the rear. He laughed. "Don't they read our dispatches? Haven't they been oriented? They must be living on the moon."

To Kluge it was all too clear that the German left flank along the Cotentin west coast had collapsed. "Someone has got to tell the Führer," he said to his chief of staff, General Günther Blumentritt, without suggesting who was to perform that unpleasant task, "that if the Americans get through at Avranches they will be out of the woods and they'll be able to do what they want."

Kluge pulled in troops from Brittany, ordering them to race to Pontaubault, four miles below Avranches, and to make sure the Americans did not seize the bridge there across the Sélune River. But when the first German elements arrived on the afternoon of July 31, they found the bridge already in American hands. Now there was nothing to stop the Americans from entering Brittany or from turning left and eastward toward the Seine River and Paris.

American armored divisions swept up more than 4,000 prisoners on the 31st; the infantry divisions behind them took an additional 3,000. Of the 28,000 enemy soldiers captured by the First Army in July, 20,000 were bagged during the last six days of the month. One German corps was smashed, another soundly defeated. Hausser's Seventh Army had been wrecked.

Cobra marked a change from slow and costly advances through the hedgerows to electrifying thrusts against defeated, disorganized and demoralized enemy forces. Allied casualties were light and morale soared. The sight of German prisoners "so happy to be captured that all they could do was giggle" dimmed the bitter memories of the costly earlier fighting.

To the Allied soldiers—racing past abandoned and destroyed equipment, past the stench and decay of dead soldiers, horses, cows and pigs—a quick end to the war appeared to be in sight.

CAUGHT IN THE CROSS FIRE

Seeking shelter during an air raid, frightened French women crouch against a wall near Caen, where thousands of civilians perished in the July 1944 fighting.

LIBERATION'S HIGH COST

During the summer of 1944, as the war raged through the northwestern corner of France, hundreds of thousands of men, women and children found themselves caught between the opposing forces. While Allied planes and artillery relentlessly bombarded towns and villages where the enemy was hiding, retreating Germans mined, burned, shelled and booby-trapped buildings, roads and bridges. Dazed civilians saw their homes and shops go up in flames, their livestock killed, their wheat fields ground to dust, and their loved ones buried alive beneath mountains of rubble. In Normandy alone nearly 187,000 buildings were damaged, 133,500 were completely demolished and 356,000 people were left homeless.

Thousands of French civilians picked up the few possessions they could carry and set off down the road to get away from the fighting. Those who were lucky rode bicycles, mules and in horse-drawn carts. But most people traveled on foot, pushing wheelbarrows or lugging their belongings on their backs. Often they did not know where they were going or even where they would find their next meal. Some holed up in trenches, tunnels, caves and quarries or slept within the solid walls of châteaux and medieval cathedrals. A few refugees even sought protection inside cemetery vaults and the padded cells of asylums. Others fled to nearby towns, villages or farms, only to be forced to flee again when the bombing and shelling caught up with them or when retreating Germans, searching for quarters, took over their shelters.

So great was the suffering that many Frenchmen were too numb to celebrate when Allied troops finally arrived to liberate them. "Some of the refugees in front of us remained impassive or stupefied in the midst of the gesticulations and cries of other inhabitants of the town," one Norman recalled. "The end of their anguish left them immobile, smiling stupidly, or lifting their arms without conviction. . . . Later, of course, we cried out with joy; but this first minute brought too much emotion. We only wanted to weep in a corner."

Straddling the pavement and the street, a disabled German tank blocks the entranceway of a shop—to the dismay of a French townswoman.

As shells fly overhead, a boy clutches his dog before shattered windows in the Brittany town of Dinard. The town was liberated by Americans in August 1944.

Rendered homeless by bombing and shelling, a little girl in Normandy pulls a cart bearing her doll and other possessions past an enormous pile of rubble.

Displaced civilians, fleeing Pont-l'Abbé on the coast of Brittany, hasten down a battle-scarred street.

Nuns evacuated from Caen receive a helping hand from men of the RAF, who drove them to Bayeux.

THE AGONIES
OF THE DISPOSSESSED

No matter where they went, the refugees could not escape the dangers and privations of war. When they were on the road, they risked stepping on German mines. And Allied planes—firing at almost every moving target—were a constant terror.

Even when the fleeing civilians managed to find a place to stay, they lived in fear and squalor. In Caen one building for 600 was invaded by 6,000; its wine cellar was so crammed that some people slept inside a wine press. Hospitals were jam-packed as well, and they were often without gas, electricity or water.

Food was so scarce that refugees had to scramble to find enough to live on. They butchered the animals killed by shells, salvaged food from wrecked stores and stole German supplies. Sometimes the fighting raged so fiercely they could not even forage for food and had to spend days without any nourishment.

With nowhere to go, a woman and her dog make a home for themselves under a roadside cart. Her farm was turned into a charred ruin by the fighting.

Elderly refugees hobble along a country road. So suddenly did the war come to their village, they barely had time to grab a few possessions before fleeing.

A bewildered girl shows the strain of fleeing from a farm near Argentan. Children were so overwhelmed by events that they often feared their liberators.

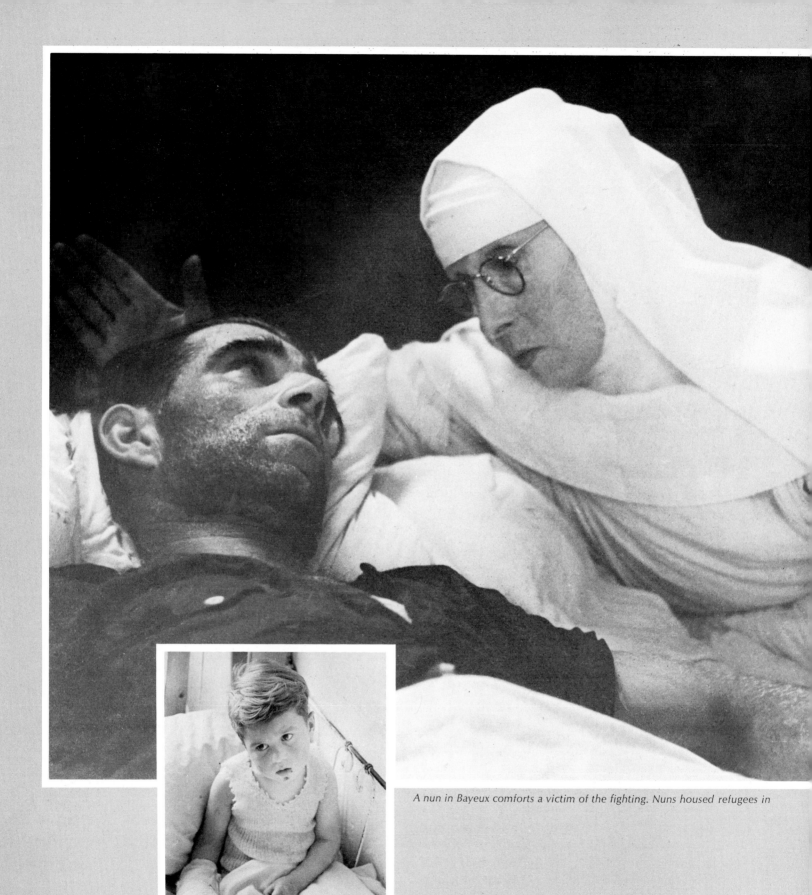

A nun in Bayeux comforts a victim of the fighting. Nuns housed refugees in

An injured boy stares listlessly from a hospital bed.

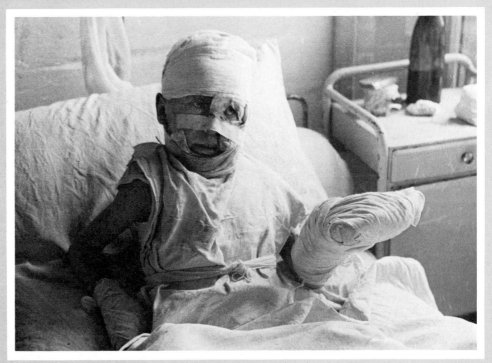
Swathed in bandages, a little boy who was severely injured by a bomb recovers in a hospital at Bayeux.

their churches and took care of the wounded.

Wounded during the battle for Argentan, a priest describes the battle he witnessed from his cathedral.

In a cave once used for brewing beer and more recently for hiding valuables from the Germans, a woman cooks for her husband.

Townspeople in a 19th Century fort at Tours share a meal while American and German forces battle over the city in August of 1944.

Exhausted civilians catch up on sleep in the solidly built cloister of the cathedral of Caen, while the battle rages outside in the streets.

A nun in the hospital ward of the quarry of Fleury-sur-Orne near Caen watches over a cauldron of soup while men chop wood.

In a crowded soup kitchen in Dreux, refugees
—most of them from the Paris area—are
served food from captured German stores.

Women taking shelter in a château chat with
a visiting RAF medical officer. The refugees slept
on thick piles of straw covering the floor.

A grieving woman is led away by a neighbor after coming back to her home in Saint-Marcouf and finding the body of her husband, who had been killed by a shell.

A handful of the 20,000 inhabitants of Laval who had fled to nearby farms return with their furniture.

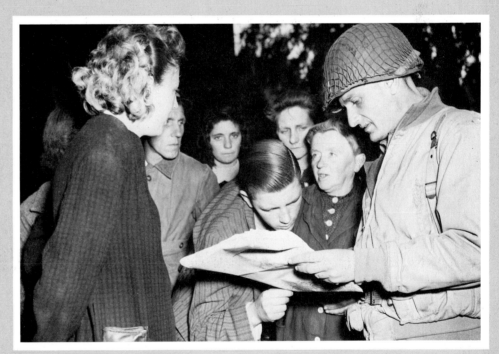

A refugee points out his village on a map to a U.S. officer who was arranging his journey home.

A DESOLATION
IN COMING HOME

For the dispossessed there was no greater disappointment after the joy of liberation than to return to their towns and cities and find ruins where their houses had once stood. Bulldozers, shoving the wreckage into mountainous heaps, sometimes made it impossible for previous residents to salvage anything at all of their former lives.

Many rushed to their towns and villages only to discover that the mines had not been cleared away from the streets and that they would have to wait for engineers to remove them. The citizens of Saint-Lô were barred from entering their city for eight weeks. And what they saw when at last they reentered was a complete wasteland. Saint-Lô was not the only town so ravaged. Of Normandy's 3,400 other towns and villages, 586 had to be completely rebuilt following liberation.

In the liberated city of Troyes, French girls tear down a German sign.

A Normandy villager (in cap) tells Americans why he killed the German on the ground—the German had treated him poorly, forcing him to work for a pittance.

Bradley's *Cobra* operation tore a funnel-shaped hole in the German defenses that was 10 miles wide at Avranches and narrowed to a single road and a bridge at Pontaubault. Through this opening poured more and more U.S. troops. The breakout was accompanied by a shift in the high command. Bradley took over the newly formed U.S. Twelfth Army Group, which included the First Army, under the soft-spoken infantry expert Lieut. General Courtney H. Hodges, and the Third Army, under the fiery and aggressive General Patton. Montgomery's command, the Twenty-first Army Group, now consisted solely of British and Canadian troops.

The Third Army swung into action on August 1. The new force included the VIII Corps—already in action under Patton's direction—and the XV Corps. In 48 hours, Patton squeezed two armored divisions through the bottleneck formed by the one road and bridge at Pontaubault. On their heels came other units, wriggling along the highways clogged with debris and dead animals, past wrecked vehicles and stacks of hastily abandoned mines, and through shattered villages and towns.

There was nothing to stop Patton's surge. The only weapon the Germans could bring to bear initially was the badly weakened Luftwaffe. By a superhuman effort, German pilots made the attempt, repeatedly strafing and bombing the tightly packed units moving down the corridor from Avranches. But the German aerial attack failed to halt the massive flow of men and machines from the Cotentin to the verdant, wide-open countryside to the south.

As the American tanks and motorized units burst out of the narrow end of the funnel and charged into Brittany *(map, page 90),* the whole character of the fighting abruptly changed. "Suddenly the war became fun," war correspondent James Wellard later wrote. "It became exciting, carnivalesque, tremendous. It became victorious and even safe."

Patton and his armored-division commanders were old cavalrymen, brought up in the hell-for-leather tradition by which horsemen rode off in a cloud of dust and chased the enemy over the landscape while higher headquarters wondered where they were. The armored divisions traveled so fast that they frequently ran out of the range of radios, and supply outfits had to struggle to catch up with tanks and motorized infantry and service them on the run. "Within a couple of days we were passing out rations like Santa Claus

3

THE GERMANS ON THE RUN

on his sleigh, with both giver and receiver on the move," said one armored-division officer. "The trucks were like a band of stagecoaches making a run through Indian country. We got used to keeping the wheels going, disregarding the snipers and hoping we wouldn't get lost or hit."

Patton's orders from Bradley were to overrun the Brittany peninsula and capture some ports to ease the critical supply situation. Two crack armored divisions were assigned this mission. The 6th Armored Division was to dash out to the end of the peninsula and try to grab Brest, Brittany's biggest port; meanwhile, the 4th Armored Division would slice down to the southwest to seal off the peninsula and occupy Lorient and Vannes in the Quiberon Bay area, where the Allies planned to construct a huge supply complex.

The dash across Brittany was a brilliant but bitterly frustrating operation. The 4th Armored raced 40 miles from Pontaubault on the afternoon of August 1 and bumped into a hastily formed German defensive unit outside Rennes. Refusing to be slowed down, the division swept around the western edge of the city in two parallel columns, and the 8th Division's 13th Infantry Regiment came down from Avranches to clear out the Germans. The defenders made a show of force, but seeing the hopelessness of their situation, they prepared to leave, burning everything they could not take with them. As American troops moved into the city and accepted the kisses and wine of the liberated and overjoyed inhabitants, the Germans, in trucks and on foot, moved out the other side. By confining their movements to small back-country roads, they avoided the Americans and escaped to Saint-Nazaire, 65 miles to the south.

Below Rennes, the 4th Armored Division's commander, Major General John S. Wood, halted the division and pondered his next move. Wood's orders from Patton called for him to turn southwest and go streaking down to Lorient. But Wood was tempted to turn east and head for central France, where the main battle with the Germans was sure to occur.

While Wood was considering this alternative, his immediate superior, General Middleton, the capable, meticulous VIII Corps commander, suddenly appeared at Wood's command post. "What's the matter?" Middleton asked facetiously. "Have you lost your division?"

"No," Wood replied. "They"—meaning the Allied high command—"are winning the war the wrong way." The right way, as far as he was concerned, was to turn to the east and outflank the Germans.

Middleton decided on a compromise. He told Wood to go as far as the Vilaine River, southwest of Rennes, and await further orders. But when Patton's chief of staff, Major General Hugh J. Gaffey, learned of this development, he immediately ordered Wood to follow the original plan and proceed to Lorient as fast as possible. The delay cost Wood a whole day and enabled the German garrison at Lorient to get ready to meet and turn back his assault.

The 6th Armored Division also lost a crucial day through a similar mix-up. The division commander, Major General Robert W. Grow, was at a crossroad in Pontaubault on August 1, directing his tanks and troops through the bottleneck at the bridge, when Patton arrived on the scene. Patton said he had bet Montgomery £5 that American troops would be in Brest, 200 miles away, by Saturday night, only four days off, and he ordered Grow to hit the road at once.

Grow asked Patton whether he should worry about anything except Brest and was told no. "Take Brest," Patton said simply. Grow quickly sent his troops racing westward toward the vital port.

Unaware of Patton's order to Grow, Middleton began to fume. He wondered why Grow had bypassed Saint-Malo, a small but valuable port just around the corner from Pontaubault, with scarcely a sidelong glance. Middleton sent Grow a note by messenger ordering him to divert the 6th Armored from the drive toward Brest and to take Saint-Malo.

Bitterly disappointed over being diverted from their exciting dash toward Brest, Grow and his chief of staff were sitting in the sun drinking coffee in a wheat field, discussing plans for an attack toward Saint-Malo, when once again Patton appeared. It was evident at a glance that Grow was not driving toward Brest, and Patton was angry. "What in hell are you doing sitting here?" he shouted in his high-pitched voice. "I thought I told you to go to Brest."

Grow said his advance had been halted.

"On what authority?" Patton demanded.

"Corps order, sir." Grow's chief of staff handed Middleton's message to Patton. "I'll see Middleton," said Patton. "You go ahead where I told you to go."

The halt had cost the 6th Armored 24 hours. With the

help of Frenchmen who pointed out where small groups of Germans were hiding, the troops bypassed potential opposition and reached the outskirts of Brest by Sunday, August 6—too late for Patton to win his bet.

Grow ordered Combat Command B of his division to attack toward Brest. The unit ran into heavy opposition, and Grow decided to see whether he could persuade the Germans to surrender before a major battle developed. He sent an officer and a sergeant in a white-draped jeep to deliver a surrender ultimatum to the German commander, Colonel Hans von der Mosel, at Brest.

Mosel refused to surrender, and the 6th Armored prepared to attack the city. The next day, the Brest defenders were reinforced by the German 2nd Parachute Division under Lieut. General Herman B. Ramcke, who replaced Mosel as fortress commander. Meanwhile, another German reinforcement unit blundered into the rear of the 6th Armored. This outfit turned out to be the better part of an infantry division sent from Morlaix, near Brittany's north coast. A confused and furious battle erupted, and all but a few of the infantrymen were prevented from reaching Brest.

The 6th Armored now turned again to attack the city. The Germans, under orders from Hitler to deny the port to the Allies at all cost, resisted fiercely. Elements of the 8th Infantry Division were brought up to help out. It would be six weeks before Brest fell, and the 6th Armored would be relieved and two divisions called in to join the 8th Division before the Germans finally yielded. As for the port, the Germans left it completely wrecked.

Meanwhile, at the base of the Brittany peninsula, infantrymen of the 83rd Division had launched an attack on Saint-Malo, and a bitter fight had developed. The commander of the heavily fortified town, Colonel Andreas von Aulock, promised Kluge, the Army Group B commander, to make it "another Stalingrad."

Asked by the French inhabitants to spare the historic port town—home of the 16th Century explorer Jacques Cartier—Aulock referred the request to Hitler. Hitler replied that in warfare there was no such thing as a historic city. "You will fight to the last man," he said. Aulock ordered all civilians to evacuate the town. A long and pathetic parade of men, women and children carrying suitcases and pushing carts and baby carriages came over into the American lines.

The Germans occupied strong defensive positions in a fortified complex covering Saint-Malo and the surrounding area. The defenses were dominated by a heavily reinforced 18th Century fort known as the Citadel, which was dug into a rocky promontory near the harbor. German coastal batteries on the nearby island of Cézembre opened fire on the Americans on the outskirts of town, and a shell knocked the spire off the Saint-Malo cathedral. Fires broke out; Saint-Malo burned for more than a week, and demolitions set by the Germans destroyed the port, quays, locks, breakwaters and harbor machinery.

As troops of the 83rd Division moved in, they faced belts of double-apron barbed wire, large minefields, rows of steel gates, antitank obstacles, underground pillboxes, iron rail fences and concrete bunkers. Bullets and shell fragments were so heavy in the town's streets that engineers dynamited passageways for the infantry to advance from house to house. Ten artillery battalions, including 8-inch guns and 240mm howitzers, joined with tank destroyers and tanks to pound German strong points. Medium bombers attacked Aulock's Citadel headquarters but had little effect on the underground installations.

The Americans captured a German chaplain and prevailed upon him to try to persuade Aulock to give up. The chaplain was permitted by the Germans to visit their commander, but he made no headway. "A German soldier does not surrender," Aulock said.

With the failure of the chaplain's peacemaking efforts, the mayor of the neighboring village of Saint-Servan-sur-Mer came forward with the information that he knew a French woman who had been on intimate terms with Aulock. The woman was now in Allied territory, and the mayor suggested that she make a telephone call to the German colonel. A telephone line from Saint-Servan to the Citadel was still in service, and a call was duly placed. But Aulock, unmoved by romantic considerations, sent word that he was too busy to come to the phone.

Deep inside the Citadel, Aulock told his troops: "Anyone deserting or surrendering is a common dog." For more than a week, the bombardments and attacks went on. On August 11, medium bombers dropped 1,000-pound bombs on the Citadel. Then troops of the 83rd attacked with Bangalore torpedoes and flamethrowers; demolition charges, mortar

Along the bomb-ravaged road between Caen and Falaise, a Canadian casualty is tended by a medic while a German tank burns only a few yards away. In August 1944, fighting raged along the 21-mile-long road from Caen to Falaise for nine days as the Canadian First Army battered its way through the tough German defenses. The Canadian advance—which produced more than 2,000 casualties—was, in General Eisenhower's eyes, a remarkable achievement. "Ten feet gained on the Caen sector," the Supreme Commander said, "was equivalent to a mile elsewhere."

and artillery fire were used, all to no avail. On the 13th, tank destroyers, artillery and medium bombers struck; two days later, following another medium-bomber attack, infantry assault teams were driven off by machine-gun fire. Finally, on August 17, just before planes were to attack with napalm, a white flag was raised over the Citadel.

The Brittany campaign had liberated thousands of square miles and thousands of joyous Frenchmen, but it failed to secure the supply ports that were its main objective. With troops and supplies piling up in England for delivery to Allied forces on the Continent, the failure to capture even a single port intact was a major frustration. For the time being, however, this concern was obscured by momentous developments to the east.

On August 5 the Third Army's XV Corps, under Major General Wade H. Haislip, had emerged from the bottleneck at Pontaubault and headed southeast for Mayenne and Laval. The XV Corps' drive was part of a plan devised by

General Montgomery as U.S. troops were breaking out of Normandy. The operation's success confronted the Germans with two poor alternatives. They could pull troops from the Caen sector to plug the gap at Avranches or they could go on making an all-out defense in the Caen area. If they chose to weaken the Caen defenses, they would give the British and Canadians a chance to break through in that sector, and if they decided to keep their troops there, they would face being cut off by the XV Corps' swing eastward.

In less than half a day, the XV Corps covered 30 miles, with the Germans nowhere in sight. Haislip's tanks pushed 45 miles more to Le Mans within the next three and a half days. The American troops were now 85 miles southeast of Avranches and threatening the two German armies west of the Seine with encirclement.

Hitler still clung to the notion that the situation could be stabilized. He believed that Kluge could counterattack, regain Avranches and restore the old Normandy front. Then the static warfare that had hemmed in the Allies and kept

them confined to a relatively small area through June and most of July could be renewed, and the Americans who had already passed through the bottleneck at Pontaubault would be cut off and could be dealt with in good time.

Hitler ordered Kluge to attack to the west through Mortain to reach the coast at Avranches, thereby separating the U.S. First and Third Armies, and then to turn north and throw the Allies into the sea. The Führer even decided to release some of his carefully hoarded divisions from the Pas-de-Calais and bring additional units up from southern France for the attack.

By August 6, four panzer divisions had been assembled and were ready to strike toward Avranches. "The decision in the Battle of France depends on the success of the attack," the Führer announced in an order of the day. The Germans, he said, had "a unique opportunity, which will never return, to drive into an extremely exposed enemy area and thereby change the situation completely."

Standing directly in the path of the Germans was the American 30th Infantry Division, a veteran outfit. Its men had spent a grueling 49 days fighting in the hedgerows and had been sent to a rest area at Tessy-sur-Vire after *Cobra*. Now they had moved into the Mortain area to relieve the 1st Division, which had been ordered southward to protect the flank of Haislip's rapidly advancing XV Corps. The 30th Division had barely taken over its new sector when a warning message, based on intercepts of German radio traffic deciphered by the British code-breaking system, *Ultra*, arrived from VII Corps headquarters. "Enemy counterattack

expected vicinity Mortain . . . within twelve hours." Twenty minutes later, around midnight, the Germans struck.

The first intimation the 30th Division troops had that the attack was under way came from the rumble of tanks moving north of the town. The motors did not sound like those of American tanks. Artillery battalions quickly began to fire at the noises in the darkness at a range of 5,000 yards, which was soon reduced to 1,000.

One of the chief German objectives was Hill 317, just east of Mortain, which was the key to the entire area because of the excellent observation it afforded. The hill was held by the 2nd Battalion of the 120th Infantry Regiment.

When daylight broke on August 7, the troops on the hill discovered that the Germans had surrounded them. By 11 o'clock the Americans were in need of food, medical supplies and ammunition. Yet they were cut off and would have to wait several days before being rescued. They came to be known as the "Lost Battalion."

North of Mortain the panzers penetrated seven miles, but fearful of Allied air power, they halted at daybreak, pulled off the road and took cover under camouflage nets. At Saint-Barthélemy, 50 tanks accompanied by infantry over-ran two companies of the 30th Division's 117th Regiment. To the south of Mortain, in the Romagny area, panzers came within 250 yards of a regimental command post.

On the road to Avranches, the Germans penetrated four miles before being stopped by P-47s and rocket-firing Typhoons. The attackers were perilously close to breaking through the 30th Division—so close that General Hobbs, the division commander, could later say, "with a heavy onion breath the Germans would have achieved their objective." General Bradley immediately ordered six divisions brought into the area to reinforce the 30th and alerted still another division for possible commitment.

The Germans had been told by their weather forecasters to expect a heavy fog on the morning of August 7, and they were counting on it to conceal their movements. But the day dawned bright and clear, and they were forced by overwhelming Allied air power to hide in the forests under camouflage nets. Roaring overhead by the hundreds, the Allied fighter-bombers bombed and strafed concentrations of vehicles. "The activities of the fighter-bombers are

GERMAN FORCES

ALLIED FORCES

0   40

Scale of Miles

Following the breakout from the Normandy hedgerow country at the beginning of August 1944, troops of the U.S. Third Army dashed 85 miles to the southeast from Avranches. Meanwhile, the Canadian First Army, the British Second Army and the American First Army pressed in on the Germans from the north and west. The combined actions of these three armies threatened the German Fifth Panzer and Seventh Armies with encirclement, but Hitler, who was determined to drive a wedge between the American forces, ordered his Seventh Army to counterattack to the west through Mortain toward Avranches. The attack succeeded only in making the Germans more vulnerable to the threatened encirclement.

almost unbearable," Lieut. General Hans von Funck, the 47th Panzer Corps' commander, reported to Kluge at Army Group B. "We could do nothing against them, we could make no further progress," said Major General Heinrich von Lüttwitz, the 2nd Panzer Division's commander.

Clearly, the counterattack had failed. On August 8 the Canadians launched an attack down the Caen-Falaise road spearheaded by 600 tanks. The assault penetrated the German defenses for three miles and raised the specter of a linkup with Haislip's forces in the south that would completely cut off the Germans. Kluge thought it madness to go on sticking his head deeper into the noose at Mortain. He must pull out now or face the possibility that all of Army Group B would be destroyed.

The fighting continued inconclusively around Mortain throughout August 8. The positions remained largely unchanged, and on August 9 Hitler ordered a stronger attack toward Avranches. His officers in the field were appalled. The Seventh Army chief of staff, Brigadier General Rudolph-Christoph Gersdorff, later called the order "the apex of conduct of a command ignorant of front line conditions, taking upon itself the right to judge the situation from East Prussia." The Seventh Army commander, General Hausser, said bitterly: "This will be the death blow not only to the Seventh Army but to the entire Wehrmacht in the West."

Meanwhile, the embattled Lost Battalion was still holding out under intense pressure. The Germans had tried to dislodge the Americans by assault, but the slopes were too steep and the defensive fire too strong. Twice the Germans sent parties up the hill with white flags to demand surrender, and twice the Americans refused.

Two light planes tried to drop supplies to the men by parachute, but German antiaircraft fire chased them away. Several C-47 cargo planes then dropped food and ammunition. Using shells normally employed to scatter propaganda leaflets to the enemy, artillery units fired bandages, adhesive tape and morphine to the beleaguered troops. French civilians living in the single farmhouse on the hill helped out by sharing their few chickens, potatoes and cabbages.

Not until August 11—with the threat to their rear growing by the hour—did the Germans decide to break off the Mortain attack and withdraw from around the hill. The Americans had suffered 300 casualties, but 370 survivors walked down the hill. The men had held off the Germans for five days, and their observations of enemy movements had made it possible for Allied planes and guns to exact a heavy toll of enemy troops and weapons, including almost 100 tanks.

Meanwhile, Bradley had ordered Haislip to turn north after capturing Le Mans (map, opposite), and his tanks were now streaking toward Alençon. On August 12 they went roaring past the town, and the next day they came within sight of Argentan. The corps commander was sure he could go all the way to Falaise and link up with the Canadians pushing toward Falaise from the north; together they could prevent the escape of the two German armies in Normandy.

But then, in one of the most controversial orders of the War, General Bradley told Haislip to halt where he was. All sorts of explanations were later advanced for the failure to close the gap. Bradley said he wanted to avoid a head-on collision between Americans and Canadians and a "calamitous battle between friends." He pointed out that Allied planes had dropped time bombs in the gap—land mines that were set to explode where Haislip's men would pass. Ultra intercepts indicated that the Germans might attack Haislip from the rear; Bradley was therefore concerned lest the XV Corps get separated too widely from the First Army to the west, thus allowing space for the Germans to get through. He also feared that Haislip's corps might cross the boundary separating Montgomery's Twenty-first Army Group from Bradley's Twelfth Army Group. It was necessary, Bradley felt, to await Montgomery's invitation to penetrate farther into the zone reserved for British-Canadian operations. No such invitation was forthcoming.

Bradley went on to make the point that the German divisions inside the unclosed pocket were about to stampede through the Argentan-Falaise gap and might trample any thin line of American troops that could be established there. He preferred, he said, "a solid shoulder at Argentan to a broken neck at Falaise."

Montgomery's failure to invite Bradley into his zone may have stemmed from the fact that the Canadians were already preparing to resume their attack from the north toward Falaise. The attack was launched on August 14. The way was opened by a massive air bombardment at night.

AN AMERICAN BLITZKRIEG

Pausing at Orleans, France, on August 17, 1944, American officers watch through field glasses as an M10 tank destroyer fires across the Loire at a German tank.

GENERAL PATTON'S SPECTACULAR DRIVE

When Lieut. General George S. Patton Jr. hurled his newly activated Third Army southward from Normandy through the gap at Avranches on the first day of August, 1944, he unleashed an American blitzkrieg that would take its place among the War's most spectacular campaigns. While the VIII Corps raced westward 200 miles to reach the coveted port of Brest in six days, tanks of the XV Corps wheeled to the southeast, then turned north to help block the escape of more than 60,000 Germans in the Argentan-Falaise pocket. Meanwhile, the XX Corps and the XII Corps swung farther south for parallel sweeps along the Loire River. "The whole Western Front has been ripped open," German Field Marshal Günther von Kluge frantically radioed Hitler as his shattered Seventh Army reeled back across the Seine.

Patton was possessed with what General Dwight D. Eisenhower termed "an extraordinary and ruthless driving power." The flamboyant general believed that destiny had chosen him to be a great warrior. He customarily wore a lacquered helmet liner and ivory-handled pistols and practiced making ferocious faces in the mirror. He sought to emulate Napoleon's military successes in his campaigns and studied the military feats of Alexander the Great, Julius Caesar and William Tecumseh Sherman. He lived by three maxims: "An ounce of sweat is worth a gallon of blood," "Attack! Attack! Attack!" and Stonewall Jackson's "Never take counsel of your fears."

The maxims paid off. Patton pushed his armored spearheads up to 70 miles a day, bypassed centers of resistance and ordered his men to "continue until gasoline is exhausted, then proceed on foot." By the end of August the Third Army had swept eastward 400 miles to Verdun and had reached the Meuse River, liberating almost 50,000 square miles of territory in the process.

Patton had hoped to reach the Rhine by the first week of September, before enemy forces had time to regroup. From there, he could bring the blitzkrieg home to Berlin. But then something happened over which he had no control: he ran out of gas.

An MP waves on a convoy laden with supplies. By August 31 the Third Army drive (below) had reached Brest in the west and Verdun in the east.

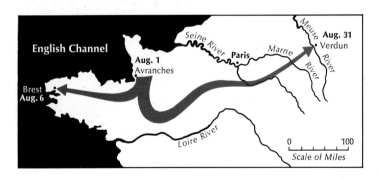

With his top subordinates and his English bull terrier Willie, Third Army commander George S. Patton Jr. waits for Eisenhower to show up for a meeting.

Townspeople of Saint-Brieuc in Brittany welcome the crew of a Third Army tank, still bearing steel blades for slicing through Normandy hedgerows.

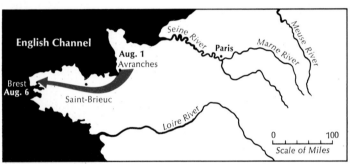

With orders from Patton to take Brest—200 miles away—the VIII Corps drove south from Avranches and west across Brittany in less than a week.

A U.S. infantryman takes aim at a sniper during street fighting in Saint-Malo on August 8. The infantry followed up the tanks and cleared out cities and towns.

The smoke of battle hangs low over a highway as a Third Army tank on its way into Dreux, just west of Paris, rolls past wrecked German armor.

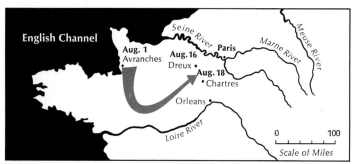

By the middle of August, Patton's forces had pushed to a north-south line cutting through Chartres, bringing them within 20 miles of the Seine River.

Citizens of Chartres celebrate liberation as Major General Lindsay M. Silvester,

commander of the XX Corps' 7th Armored Division, waves from his armored car on August 16. The Germans held out in parts of the town for two more days.

Accompanied by infantry, a XX Corps tank rolls across the French countryside near Montereau on August 25, 1944. Of Patton's nine divisions, six were infantry.

With German machine-gun fire spraying the water around them, U.S. Army engineers ferry a vehicle on a pontoon across the Seine at Montereau.

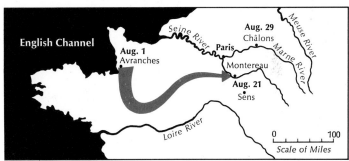

By August 25 the Third Army had bypassed Paris and crossed the Seine River. The objective was now the German border, only 200 miles away.

RUNNING OUT OF GAS WITH VICTORY IN THE AIR

The Third Army's lightning advance consumed between 500,000 and 600,000 gallons of gasoline every 50 miles. As the army raced eastward, supply lines became stretched to the breaking point.

Special convoys were organized, but the transport trucks used more than 300,000 gallons of gas a day. Patton arranged for Air Transport Command C-47s to shuttle supplies—more than 500 tons on a single day. Enemy supplies helped—100,000 gallons of gas found at Châlons-sur-Marne and 37 carloads of gas and oil at Sens. And Patton pretended not to notice when his men raided other Allied units for fuel.

As August drew to a close, however, most of Patton's gasoline was diverted to the First Army in the north. On August 31 gas delivery ended, and the Third Army ground to a halt. In the first week of September it would start again—but, as Patton angrily pointed out, only after the enemy had been given time to gather its forces.

While an amused Frenchman looks on, the crew of a Third Army half-track consumes Army rations and some French bread in the streets of Verdun.

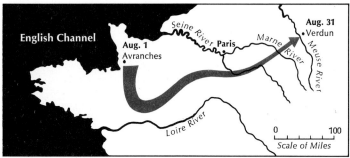

Undaunted by dwindling supplies of gasoline, the Third Army rolled on to Verdun and the Meuse before being halted abruptly by empty gas tanks.

Out of gasoline, dejected Third Army soldiers rest beside their half-track at the foot of a gigantic Verdun memorial to soldiers who died during World War I.

4

During the weeks following D-Day in Normandy, before the Allied armies broke out of their embattled beachhead, their commanders often looked wistfully south to Italy and North Africa, where U.S., Free French and British forces were hastily making preparations to invade France's Mediterranean coast. This operation, code-named *Anvil,* was to be a mighty assault on the scale of the Normandy and Sicily landings: an armada of 880 ships, preceded and protected by 2,000 bombers and fighter planes, would on the first day put ashore some 94,000 troops (and 367,000 within one month), whose mission was to drive due north up the Rhone River Valley with all possible speed. At the very least, the bold thrust would relieve German pressure on the Normandy beachhead. If all went as planned, the forces from Normandy and from southern France would complete the liberation of France by autumn.

But *Anvil*'s background did not inspire confidence in its future. Dogged by supply shortages, and by plain bad luck, the operation had repeatedly been delayed and altered. Worse, there had been bitter staff-level arguments over the strategic merits of the invasion—arguments that put terrible strains on relations between *Anvil*'s American backers and its British opponents. Worst of all, the opposition was led by a man so powerful, so eloquent and so stubborn that the invasion might well be scrubbed before the troops boarded their ships for southern France. That man was Prime Minister Winston Churchill.

The idea of invading southern France was first suggested officially in August 1943, four months after planning for the Normandy invasion had begun. The Combined Chiefs of Staff proposed the operation as a small-scale diversion to help the Normandy assault: a modest force would land in the south at the same time Normandy was invaded, thereby pinning down German units that might otherwise reinforce the defenders up north. However, when the Big Three met in November at Teheran, Stalin urged that *Anvil* be increased to a large-scale diversion, and President Roosevelt supported him. Churchill, outvoted, agreed to the change. But soon he began working against the operation through the British Chiefs of Staff, for it was obvious that *Anvil*'s added strength would have to be drawn from the Allied armies campaigning in Italy, stripping them of the surplus

SOUTHERN FRANCE'S D-DAY

manpower needed to mount one of his own pet strategies.

Basically, Churchill wanted to use those troops to open an entirely new major theater in Europe—one that would further Britain's interests in the eastern Mediterranean. He argued for a strong Allied drive north from Italy into Yugoslavia through the Alpine pass known as the Ljubljana Gap—"that gap," said Eisenhower, "whose name I can't even pronounce." These forces, perhaps with aid from amphibious landings at the head of the Adriatic, would then drive north to Vienna, blocking the westward advance of the Soviet armies and Soviet Communism. Whatever the merits of this plan, the Americans rejected it because of the mountainous terrain, and because they saw the Balkan route as a politically motivated detour that would do nothing to shorten the War. They considered a large-scale version of *Anvil* essential to the success of the Normandy invasion and not, as Churchill insisted, an unnecessary duplication of effort.

In spite of Churchill's misgivings, plans for *Anvil* went forward. The U.S. Seventh Army, most of whose troops had been parceled out among other forces after the Sicily victory, was revitalized, and it was decided that for the invasion Lieut. General Mark W. Clark, who was then commanding the Fifth Army in Italy, would succeed General Patton as Seventh Army commander. In December 1943 Clark called in the commander of his 3rd Infantry Division, Major General Lucian K. Truscott Jr., and appointed him to *Anvil*'s most important field command—leading the assault. Jut-jawed, squint-eyed and perpetually scowling, Truscott was a tough, outspoken, aggressive soldier almost universally admired by his men and his superiors.

Truscott, who had been a cavalry lieutenant colonel at the start of the War, was a perfect choice to lead the invasion spearhead. His credentials included a wealth of experience in amphibious operations. In 1942 he had studied the methods of the British Commandos, accompanied them on the ill-fated Dieppe raid and helped organize the commando-like U.S. Rangers. He later distinguished himself as a task force commander in the invasion of North Africa and as a division commander in Sicily and Italy; during those campaigns he forged his 3rd Infantry Division into one of the great combat outfits of the War.

While Truscott and Clark continued fighting their way up the Italian boot, the Seventh Army opened a secret headquarters in a sprawling Moorish-style school on the outskirts of Algiers. The *Anvil* planning staff established liaison with the Navy, the Services of Supply and the Army Air Forces. They also arranged for close contact with the Free French forces, most of whom would follow Truscott's spearhead ashore as an integral force in order to avoid language problems in combat. To select a landing area, the planners systematically sifted through masses of photographs, records and intelligence reports on France's southern coastline and its defenses.

There were two logical target areas, but both had disadvantages. The first was a 45-mile stretch of coast midway between Marseilles and the Spanish border that had the finest landing beaches in southern France. But there was no major port in the area. Moreover, this part of the French coast was out of the range of Allied tactical aircraft based in Italy, Corsica and Sardinia. The second choice would have been the beaches just west of Marseilles, a port with a handling capacity of 20,000 tons a day and the hub of a road and rail network that led to the Rhone Valley. However, the marshy Rhone delta that enveloped Marseilles would cause many landing problems.

The planners therefore looked farther east to a 45-mile stretch of the famed Riviera coast between the Bay of Cavalaire and the anchorage at Agay (map, page 102). Here, too, there were disadvantages—the beaches were narrow and cramped and at intervals cliffs fronted on the sea—but on balance this was the best area that was available, and it was chosen.

In planning tactics for the invasion, the staff faced a bewildering array of imponderables. *Anvil* ranked third in priority behind the invasion of Normandy and the Italian campaign; with every essential item in short supply, especially landing craft, the staff had to base its plans on troops, matériel and shipping whose quantity and delivery date were at best uncertain. And since the scale of *Anvil* was constantly in doubt, the planners had to prepare several different versions of the invasion and ensuing operations—and continually update them as newer surveys were completed on German troop deployment. It was frustrating work, but the magnitude of *Anvil* was eventually settled at 10 divisions, which gave the Seventh Army a solid basic plan for the main assault and a number of preliminary attacks.

For all practical purposes, the mounting of *Anvil* could not begin until the fall of Rome freed the seasoned combat divisions that Truscott would lead in the landings. But the road to Rome was blocked—interminably, it seemed—by resolute German defenses at Monte Cassino, north of Naples. In an attempt to break the bottleneck, Churchill created another one: he persuaded the Combined Chiefs to outflank Monte Cassino with an ill-starred amphibious landing 70 miles north at Anzio. Launched on January 22, 1944, the operation went so poorly that a month later Truscott, whose 3rd Division had led the first wave ashore, was promoted to commander of the VI Corps in the hope that he would break out of the besieged beachhead. It was also decided that General Clark was too valuable in Italy to be spared for the invasion of southern France; he was replaced as commander of the Seventh Army by Major General Alexander M. Patch, a veteran of the fighting on Guadalcanal. And since the Anzio operation had tied up landing craft that might have been used for *Anvil,* the Combined Chiefs were forced to postpone the landings in southern France.

The impasses at Anzio and Monte Cassino were finally broken in May, and then events moved swiftly. On June 4 the Allies took Rome; two days later Normandy was invaded, and on June 11 Truscott was ordered to start preparing for *Anvil* with three divisions of his choice.

Truscott chose two of the most experienced divisions in Italy. One was his old 3rd Division, now under the command of Major General John W. O'Daniel, a hard-bitten soldier aptly nicknamed Iron Mike, who keyed up his troops to fight the Germans by shouting, "Hate 'em! Hate 'em!" The other outfit was the 45th Division under Major General William W. Eagles, whose mild, professorial appearance belied his uncompromising toughness. Truscott considered both these selections obvious, but his third choice—the 36th Division—was not. The 36th had twice been badly mauled in the Italian campaign and was led by a new commander, Major General John E. Dahlquist, who had no combat experience at the head of a division. But the 36th had redeemed itself at Anzio, and Truscott chose it "because of its outstanding performance during the action following the breakout from the beachhead." These divisions, the nucleus of Truscott's revamped VI Corps, were

The Allied invasion of southern France got under way on August 15, 1944, when French commandos landed at Cap Nègre and west of Cannes shortly before 2:00 a.m. with the vital mission of blocking roads leading to the beachhead area from the west and east. At 4:30 a.m., troops of the 1st Airborne Task Force were dropped 12 miles inland to seize the highway junction at Le Muy. The main assault began at 8:00 a.m., when three divisions of the American VI Corps landed in the area between Cavalaire and Agay. Troops of these units managed to push inland 10 miles the first day. On D-plus-1, they were followed by the French II Corps, which came ashore near Saint-Tropez, over beaches already secured by the U.S. 3rd Division, then swung west to march on Toulon and Marseilles.

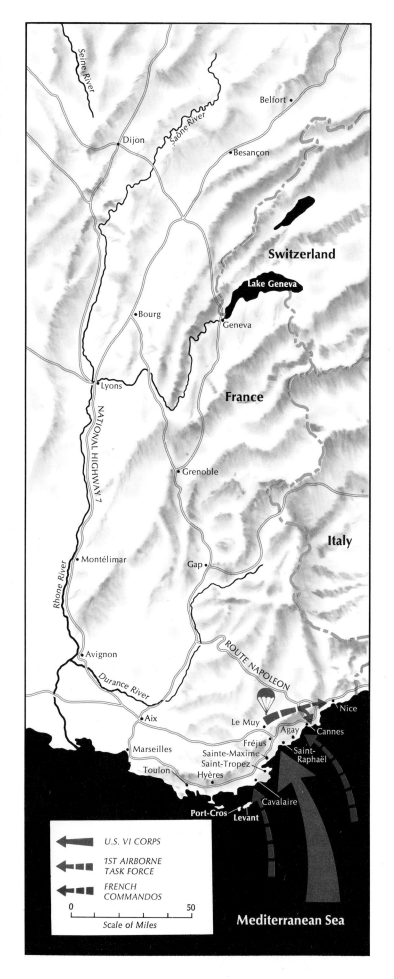

withdrawn from the line one by one and sent to the Naples area for invasion training.

On June 15 Truscott was called to Algiers to meet General Patch, the new head of the Seventh Army. Patch was a talented administrator who complemented Truscott's dynamic leadership in battle with organizing skill, patience for detail and the tact of a diplomat. "I was fully aware of his fine reputation," Truscott later wrote; on reporting to Patch, Truscott found him to be "thin and wiry, simple in dress and forthright in manner—obviously keenly intelligent with a dry Scottish sense of humor."

Patch made a different impression on his other top subordinate, General Jean de Lattre de Tassigny, whom Charles de Gaulle had appointed commander of *Anvil*'s Free French forces. De Lattre found Patch to be "deeply religious, of mystic turn of mind." Patch had shown his reverence on a hot day in Algiers when he was disconsolate because the invasion was apparently being argued to death. "With emotion," de Lattre later recalled, "he took from the drawer of his desk a box of sweets that had come from home that morning and offered them to me as if our mutual disappointment had opened his family circle to me, and said, 'Ah General, there's not much more we can do.' Then, after a silence: 'We must pray.' "

De Lattre himself was a formidable and courageous soldier. Imprisoned by the Germans as a dangerous French patriot, he had three times escaped and been recaptured. On his fourth attempt he was successful; he joined the Free French forces in North Africa and served with gallantry, most recently leading the hard-fought amphibious landing that resulted in the reconquest of Elba. He was proud, opinionated and something of a martinet—"a terrible man to serve," said one of his officers, who then added, "but I wouldn't care to serve under anyone else."

Predictably, Truscott and de Lattre rubbed each other the wrong way. Their first meeting was arranged by de Lattre, who invited Truscott to what turned out to be a long, stiff meal. "Conversation lagged during the luncheon," Truscott reported. "Everyone attended to the business of eating, the sounds of mastication dominating the scene. It finally came to a close and we learned the reason for the cool reception. De Lattre was in a towering rage." It seemed that Truscott had violated military protocol by inspecting some of de Lattre's troops without his personal permission and in his absence. "It was a slight to him," Truscott remarked, "and to the honor of France." De Lattre burst into an angry tirade over the matter, but Truscott cut him short, saying that "if that was all he had to discuss, we were wasting our time." Afterward, the two came to regard each other with wary respect, but it took all of Patch's diplomacy to smooth over their occasional clashes.

By early July de Lattre's forces were growing. Four Free French divisions, which had been instrumental in breaking the German line near Monte Cassino, were withdrawn from the line in Italy and put into training south of Naples.

Meanwhile, Truscott's VI Corps had been beefed up by the addition of some 10,000 American and British paratroopers, who would land behind the beaches on D-day; these troops, later designated the 1st Airborne Task Force, went into training outside Rome and were formed into an effective fighting unit in less than one month. Some of Patch's French-speaking soldiers remained in training in North Africa and would sail for France from there. Like the French units in Italy, their ranks were filled with thousands of veteran fighting men who had fled from the homeland and an enormous hodgepodge of volunteers from France's far-flung empire: Somalis, New Caledonians, Tahitians, Antilleans, Indochinese, Pondicherrians, Syrians, Lebanese, Algerians, Moroccans, Tunisians, men from French Equatorial Africa and West Africa, plus Foreign Legionnaires from a score of nations. The colonial soldiers had little in common, but all of them could be counted on to fight.

Even as preparations gained momentum, so did Churchill's efforts to abort the invasion, reduce its size or change its direction. He still insisted that the operation was "sheer folly," and that it would serve "no earthly purpose," especially since Normandy had already been invaded successfully. However, a new reason for the operation had arisen shortly after D-Day in Normandy. The U.S. Army Chief of Staff, General George C. Marshall, had flown to England on June 8 to help Eisenhower explain that more than 40 new American divisions had recently completed their training in the United States; they were ready and needed for the assault on Germany but could not be sent into action because the Normandy forces might not be able to capture and clear enough ports in northern France to handle the influx. The solution, Marshall said forcefully, was to capture Marseilles and use its fine facilities as a port of entry for divisions shipped directly from the United States. Eisenhower said he had to have Marseilles.

Churchill remained adamant. In a nonstop barrage of letters and cables, he hectored Roosevelt to abandon *Anvil*. On June 29 the President replied in a message that fairly sighed with weariness: "My dear friend, I beg you let us go ahead with our plan." Churchill replied that he was "deeply grieved," but the Combined Chiefs of Staff scheduled the operation for August 15.

Churchill continued his attack, shifting to a target more conveniently located in London—Eisenhower. Through July and into August, the Prime Minister subjected the Supreme Commander to what Ike described as one of the most severe trials of his life. Churchill wept: he charged the U.S. with "bullying" Britain by not adopting his grand strategy. He threatened: at one point he told Eisenhower that he might go to the King and "lay down the mantle of my high office," which indeed would have thrown the Allied war effort into turmoil. And that was just the beginning.

By August 1 the American armies were pouring out of the Normandy beachhead, increasing *Anvil*'s potential dramatically. If Patch's northbound Seventh Army and Patton's eastbound Third Army could link up, they would trap the enemy forces west of the Rhone and south of the Loire, forcing the Germans in France to surrender and liberating that whole immense bypassed territory in one great rush.

Churchill persevered. On August 5 he assailed Eisenhower with his most determined anti-*Anvil* argument. Arriving at Ike's advance headquarters near Portsmouth for a hastily arranged lunch, he disarmingly fed milk to the general's black kitten, Shaef, and then went on the offensive. Arguing for closer tactical connection between the two invading forces, he urged that the units assigned to the Riviera assault be sent instead to capture the ports of Brittany—Brest, Lorient and Saint-Nazaire—where he assumed "they could walk in like tourists." Such landings, he asserted, would not only open those ports for Allied use but also put troops ashore in position to strengthen the Allies' southern flank in the sweep east across France.

Eisenhower replied that the proposal was impossible. As

he later told the story, he informed Churchill that he expected the Brittany ports to be "stubbornly defended" and "effectively destroyed once we had captured them"; but "we did not expect this destruction to be so marked at Marseilles" because "capture should be so swift as to allow little time for demolition." Even Churchill's steadfast supporter, General Sir Henry Maitland Wilson, the Supreme Allied Commander in the Mediterranean theater, had said that *Anvil* could not be postponed again. But Churchill persisted mercilessly. According to Eisenhower's Naval aide, Commander Harry Butcher, "Ike said no, continued saying no all afternoon, and ended up saying no in every form of the English language at his command. . . . He was practically limp when the PM departed."

Three days later, Churchill apparently bowed to the inevitable. He cabled Roosevelt and agreed to the assault: "I pray God that you may be right." Then he went right on with his obstructive campaign. His final concession of defeat did not come until August 10, when the British Chiefs of Staff ordered General Wilson to execute the invasion as scheduled on August 15.

Those last five days capped a hectic final period of preparation for the invasion forces in dozens of encampments and staging areas up and down the Italian coast. By August 12 all of the 94,000 soldiers who would land on the Riviera beaches were crammed aboard their ships, with the largest flotilla riding at anchor in the Bay of Naples. General Patch (recently promoted to lieutenant general) and General Truscott boarded the command ship *Catoctin* with Vice Admiral Henry Kent Hewitt, whose huge Western Task Force was to deliver the Seventh Army into combat. The ships began leaving on a staggered schedule.

Late on the brilliant afternoon of August 13, the few officers in the Naples fleet who knew of Churchill's dogged opposition were amazed to see his familiar figure moving among the ships aboard a British motor launch, his pudgy fingers outthrust in his famous V-for-Victory sign. The Prime Minister, making a grand Churchillian gesture, had come to wish *bon voyage* to his least-favorite operation. The troops aboard the transports greeted him with cheers, and the men of the 3rd Division serenaded him with their marching song, "The Dog Face Soldier." Churchill beamed. There was a story that he even permitted himself a rueful joke about his long and bitter resistance to the invasion. *Anvil* had been renamed *Dragoon* on August 1 to maintain security, and the new name, Churchill said, was entirely fitting: he had, after all, been dragooned into accepting the operation.

From their scattered ports, the flotillas of the Seventh Army invasion fleet converged on their rendezvous off the coast of Corsica. Behind the ships carrying the VI Corps came the vessels bearing de Lattre's French Army B, which would start landing on the day after D-day, D-plus-1. On board, the troops received their last briefings, and unit commanders studied the latest updated intelligence reports on German troop deployments.

The Germans' static coastal defenses, known as the Mediterranean Wall, were not as formidable as those the Allies had encountered in Normandy, and German air and naval forces were negligible. But 200 guns of medium and heavy caliber had been massed in the Toulon area, with nearly as many at Marseilles, and 45 more batteries were strewn along the coast between the Rhone and Agay, some of them camouflaged as Riviera cabanas and refreshment stands. In addition, some 600 concrete pillboxes and other strongholds faced the sea between Marseilles and Nice, and the beaches were seeded with mines and anti-invasion obstacles, many of them with 75mm shells rigged to explode on contact. Inland, the flowering meadows of Provence bristled with needle-pointed pine poles designed to destroy gliders and to impale paratroopers. However, conscripted French laborers had deliberately dug only shallow postholes, so that many of the poles would topple at a touch.

These defenses and the personnel manning them were controlled by German Army Group G, headquartered near Toulouse, some 260 miles from the threatened coast. The commanding officer was General Johannes Blaskowitz, a competent, correct product of the German general staff system, whose only black mark was that he had run afoul of Adolf Hitler at the outset of the War. As commander of the army besieging Warsaw, Blaskowitz had received notice that the Führer intended to drop by for a field-kitchen meal and wanted no frills laid on. Blaskowitz, failing to realize that Hitler wanted a genuinely spartan meal, had the tables elaborately set with paper cloths and decorated with flow-

ers. The Führer arrived, took one look at the tables and stalked away indignantly without eating. "From that moment on," reported Field Marshal Albert Kesselring, "Hitler regarded Blaskowitz with suspicion."

One of the two armies in Blaskowitz' group, the Nineteenth, under Lieut. General Friedrich Wiese, held the Riviera coast; he commanded or had within calling range no less than 10 divisions. But that strength was somewhat deceptive. One of Wiese's divisions was totally occupied in the French Alps fighting strong Resistance units, some of them members of de Gaulle's formally organized FFI (Forces Françaises de l'Intérieur), others belonging to the Maquis guerrilla bands who took their name from the word for the scrubby underbrush of the French hill country. Several other divisions were of poor quality; their troops were young and inexperienced or they were heavily diluted by ragtag collections of Poles, Armenians, Georgians, Ukrainians, Azerbaijanis—soldiers who had been captured on the Eastern Front and who had opted to serve under German officers rather than waste away in prison camps or labor battalions. The abilities and the loyalties of the foreign troops were dubious at best.

However, Wiese's army was no paper tiger. Four of his divisions were highly rated formations, and Truscott took them seriously. And then there was the powerful 11th Panzer Division, with 14,000 top-quality troops and 200 tanks. At last report, the 11th Panzer had been stationed near Bordeaux, approximately 400 miles west of the attack zone, and like all of the German panzer divisions, it could not be sent into action without direct permission from Hitler himself. But the division could move quickly and hit hard whenever the order came.

Unbeknownst to the invasion forces, the Germans knew all about the attack—only the exact landing area was in doubt. German intelligence had reported large and small indications of an imminent strike by the Allies. Various French units had very suddenly been pulled out of the fighting in Italy, and the Germans were well aware of de Gaulle's pledge that the next destination of his forces would be France itself. A German agent in Naples had reported the appearance on the north Italian coast of the U.S.S. *Augusta*, a heavy cruiser with too much firepower to be sent there unless a new invasion was in the offing. And in July an

American Red Cross worker in Rome had been overheard saying, "I've got to get to Naples by August 1, because I'm going to be in on the invasion of southern France a few weeks after that."

Blaskowitz and Wiese were just as worried as Truscott about the location of the 11th Panzer Division. Blaskowitz had begged OKW, the German High Command at the Wolf's Lair in East Prussia, for permission to move the armored division to the Riviera coast, and a draft order to that effect had been prepared. But General Jodl, Hitler's operations chief, had delayed presenting the order to the Führer until the 13th of August, when he was convinced that an invasion was looming.

Hitler read the order and brightened on reaching a passage that called for "resistance by all available means" along the coast of southern France. That meant moving the 11th Panzer, and he signed the appropriate order.

Word crackled down through Hitler's elaborate chain of command to Army Group G headquarters near Toulouse. Chief of Staff Major General Heinz von Gyldenfeldt rushed into Blaskowitz' office shouting, "Here's the order! It just came through!" Moments later Gyldenfeldt was on the phone to the Nineteenth Army, informing Wiese that the 11th Panzer had been released to his command. The division was loaded on 33 trains and headed eastward on August 14, but the unit was soon forced by Allied air attacks to abandon the trains and take to the roads.

As darkness fell on the soft, fragrant Languedoc countryside, armored cars emblazoned with skulls and crossbones led the tanks of the 11th Panzer Division east toward Avignon on the Rhone. To avoid further air attacks, the division had been instructed to use back roads and to travel only at night. But Major General Wend von Wietersheim, the division commander, was in a hurry, and he ignored the orders. According to his chief of staff, the 11th Panzer raced for the Rhone with its "vehicles bristling with foliage, speeding

along the main highways in broad daylight, leaving ample space between them, darting from one place of concealment to the next."

On the evening of August 14—when Wiersheim's advance units were within 15 miles of the Rhone and, far to the north, tanks of the U.S. Third Army were driving toward Chartres—the Allied invasion fleet made its Corsica rendezvous and steamed cautiously toward the coast of southern France. As darkness fell, advance elements of the Seventh Army debarked and set out on five preliminary operations designed to pave the way for the morning assault by Truscott's main force.

French Lieut. Colonel Georges-Régis Bouvet, commander of Operation *Romeo,* set off for the shore at Cap Nègre with 800 French commandos aboard 20 landing craft; their mission was to scale a cliff 350 feet high and destroy German artillery that would otherwise bombard the left flank of Truscott's VI Corps' landings.

Ahead of the main party of French commandos, bobbing along in a rubber boat, went nine men led by Sergeant Georges du Bellocq. They were to land near Cap Nègre on the beach at Rayol and knock out German blockhouses. Somehow the little party drifted to a landing west of Rayol. Now, in the darkness, du Bellocq was obsessed with the idea of "getting the hell out of this nameless beach." Crawling, climbing, bloodying their hands on barbed-wire obstacles, the commandos finally arrived at a network of trenches that du Bellocq thought was empty—until a voice to his left called, "Ludwig! Ludwig!" Du Bellocq sent a submachine-gun burst in that direction, and the enemy soldier screamed once, then "gurgled and shut up"—the first German to die in the invasion of southern France. The sound of gunfire set off a lively fire fight—mostly among the Germans themselves. "From that moment on during the whole rest of the night," du Bellocq recalled, "the Jerries hardly left off shooting at one another."

In one of the 20 landing craft offshore, Bouvet heard the sound of the fracas and stared into the darkness, looking for a green signal that was to be flashed by one of his men ashore, marking his beach. There was no signal; either it—or his main force—was in the wrong place. The Canadian midshipman in charge of the LCI thereupon refused to take the commandos ashore. Bouvet, an experienced improviser, changed the Canadian's mind with a pistol jammed in the ribs. The landing craft touched shore a mile west of the assigned beach.

Then Bouvet and his French commandos went to work. They scaled the steep cliff, took the enemy by surprise, destroyed the gun emplacements, established a roadblock on the coastal highway, picked up du Bellocq's team and other advance units, seized Cap Nègre, killed some 300 Germans and took 700 prisoners—all this in about 12 hours while losing only 11 men killed and 50 wounded. They had established a bridgehead two miles deep and more than a mile wide, and there they stayed, awaiting troops of Truscott's VI Corps from the beachhead to the east.

A different kind of preliminary attack, code-named *Ferdinand,* was aimed at La Ciotat, between Marseilles and Toulon, where the Germans expected a major invasion to take place. Five transport planes dropped 300 life-size dummies dressed as American paratroopers and rigged with explosive charges and noisemaking equipment that simulated the sound of battle when jarred by contact with the ground. Germans of the 244th Infantry Division were fooled by the trick. Crying "Paratroopers! Paratroopers!" they encircled the invaders. When they received no answering fire, a few men prodded the dummies with fixed bayonets—only to detonate more charges. The diversionary effort was so successful that the next day it earned special mention in a broadcast by Radio Berlin; the German station denounced the fake paratrooper attack as something that "could have been contrived only by the lowest and most sinister type of Anglo-Saxon mind."

In the meantime, the American-Canadian 1st Special Service Force was staging Operation *Sitka,* 25 miles southeast of Toulon, on the picturesque, pine-clad islands of Port-Cros and Ile du Levant. Aerial photographs had shown strong artillery batteries on both islands, and some 2,000 men of the crack attack force were sent to wipe them out, even though a knowledgeable French informant insisted that the three 164mm guns on Levant had been destroyed in November 1942, when the Germans occupied the southern half of France and the French fleet was hastily scuttled in Toulon harbor. One large detachment, led in by scouts in kayaks and on electrically operated surfboards, scrambled

Hundreds of parachutes, streaming from U.S. transports on August 15, 1944—D-day in southern France—drop supplies to the 1st Airborne Task Force, whose American and British paratroopers had landed in the dark near Le Muy, 12 miles behind the invasion beaches. By the time of the supply drop, the soldiers had achieved their main objective: setting up roadblocks to keep German reinforcements from reaching the beachhead.

ashore on Levant and rushed inland without a shot being fired. They soon learned that the French informant was right; the Levant guns turned out to be dummies, skillfully fashioned from corrugated metal, wooden stakes and drainpipes. Just before dawn on August 15, the commander on Levant radioed General Patch: "Islands utterly useless. Suggest immediate evacuation. Killed: none. Wounded: two. Prisoners: 240. Enemy batteries dummies."

Soon afterward, while the troops on Levant were liquidating a last pocket of German resistance, radio contact broke off. Hours later, Patch decided to send an aide to find out what was going on. "In that case, general," said a visitor, "I wouldn't mind being in the party. It'll give me a chance to stretch my legs." The volunteer was U.S. Secretary of the Navy James Forrestal. (*Dragoon* was notable for the number of visiting dignitaries; a week later, at a critical point in the campaign, Truscott would have to take time out to entertain Eisenhower's political adviser, Ambassador Robert D. Murphy, and New York's Archbishop Francis J. Spellman.)

Meanwhile, at the opposite end of the assault area, a film star turned U.S. Navy lieutenant commander, Douglas Fairbanks Jr., presided over the mixed fortunes of Operation *Rosie,* designed to block the coastal roads from Cannes west to the invasion area. Fairbanks' forces consisted of two gunboats, a fighter-director ship with sound equipment to broadcast a recording of naval gunfire, and four fast PT boats carrying demolition teams of 67 French commandos. To distract the Germans from the commandos' mission, Fairbanks' little flotilla raced east toward Nice, making a fearful racket (and prompting Radio Berlin to announce later that Antibes and Nice had been bombarded by "four or five large battleships"). But when the commandos were put ashore well to the west of Cannes, they ran into atrocious luck. First, they stumbled into an unreported minefield, laid only a day or two before. Next, having failed to achieve their objectives, they tried to withdraw—only to be mistaken for Germans and shot up by a pair of prowling Allied fighter planes. Of the 67 Frenchmen, only 40 survived, and they were captured by the Germans.

The largest preliminary operation, code-named *Rugby,* was aimed at Le Muy, 12 miles inland from Fréjus in the eastern sector of the Allied assault area. Le Muy was an insignificant village except for the fact that two vital high-

ways converged there. At Le Muy, the Route Napoleon (handsomely paved since Napoleon used it on his return from Elba) ran northward to Grenoble, and National Highway 7 branched west from the Route Napoleon to Avignon, thence north up the Rhone Valley. By seizing Le Muy and its environs, the Seventh Army could not only prevent German reinforcements from reaching the beachheads but also hold open the routes that the VI Corps needed to exploit its landings. Thus, in the predawn hours of August 15, little Le Muy became the main objective of the big Anglo-American 1st Airborne Task Force.

Commanding the division-sized group was the youngest major general in the American Army and an extraordinary soldier: Robert T. Frederick. Of willowy build and wearing a dandified little moustache, the 37-year-old Frederick resembled—in the words of a Canadian officer—"a bloody goddamned actor." But he was a fierce and brilliant fighter. He had been wounded nine times in the War, had won many decorations and had received a rare accolade from Winston Churchill: "If we had a dozen men like him, we would have smashed Hitler in 1942."

Frederick's first paratroop wave dropped at 4:30 on the morning of D-day. Most of the units landed on or near their targets, and by 6 p.m. the force had taken several villages and thrown blockades over the road network linking the invasion coast to the interior.

Le Muy itself held out, mostly because of what Frederick deemed a halfhearted attack by the British 2nd Independent Parachute Brigade. Frederick turned the job over to his American 550th Glider Infantry Battalion, which took Le Muy by noon on D-plus-1. The linkup with troops from the invasion beaches came about an hour later, when a tank named "The Anzio Express" clanked into town. By then the Seventh Army was in business along its invasion front.

The preinvasion bombardment and the landings of Truscott's VI Corps went like clockwork. At 5:50 that morning, an hour after first light, another actor-turned-officer, French liaison officer Jean-Pierre Aumont, looked up from a landing craft off the 3rd Division beaches and saw what appeared to be "glistening drops of radium caught in the rays of the rising sun." These were the first of some 1,300 American, British and French bombers, arriving unopposed

U.S. 45th Division infantrymen stream ashore and make their way inland through an opening in the sea wall near Sainte-Maxime in August 1944. Erected by the Germans, the concrete wall was 10 feet high and six feet thick—one of the most formidable obstacles on the Riviera. After repeated air and naval bombardments failed to open a breach, U.S. engineers had to go ashore and blast a passageway through it for troops and vehicles.

from Sardinia and Corsica to pound the Riviera for the next hour and 40 minutes. The long and wide-ranging bombing attacks drove the Germans under cover and destroyed, among other things, a bridge at Pont-Saint-Esprit. This was the last of six bridges across a 30-mile stretch of the lower Rhone, and its destruction left the 11th Panzer Division stranded on the wrong side of the river. The most formidable enemy unit had to mark time until it could improvise some means of crossing the river to reach the assault area.

At precisely 7:30 the bombing ceased and the big planes disappeared in the distance. One minute passed in what seemed to be a dead silence. Then another fury was unleashed, this time from the 400 guns of the Allied warships offshore. During the next 19 minutes they fired some 16,000 shells at German batteries and strong points. On schedule at 7:50 a.m., the naval guns fell quiet and the invasion craft headed into the ground fog cloaking the beaches.

The first elements landed right on time at 8 o'clock. On the VI Corps' left, Iron Mike O'Daniel's 3rd Division hit two beaches 13 miles apart and moved to pinch off the Saint-Tropez peninsula, a pastoral patch of vineyards and olive groves cut by narrow, winding roads. The assault troops met with hardly any German opposition. A French woman, witnessing the advance from her home overlooking Cavalaire-sur-Mer, was impressed by "the deep silence, so profound that not even a leaf seemed to be rustling." When the German soldiers finally did emerge from their pillboxes, where they had holed up during the preliminary bombardment, they seemed dazed.

General O'Daniel went ashore at 10:44 a.m. and set up his command post in a barnyard nearly a mile inland. Even as local farmers were trundling out welcoming kegs of wine, O'Daniel established radio communication with a friendly force. "Hello, Bouvet," said Iron Mike. "Well, we made it." Three and a half hours later, 3rd Division units joined up with Colonel Bouvet and his commandos, who, after seizing Cap Nègre, had stoutly defended their inland roadblock against German attack.

The 3rd Division's main D-day objective was the town of Saint-Tropez. But by the time infantry units arrived there to take the town, they found that the job had been all but done for them by some paratroopers of the 1st Airborne

109

Task Force who, having been dropped far off target, had joined local Resistance fighters in seizing the town. Thus, by nightfall on D-day the 3rd Division had achieved all its objectives and taken 1,600 prisoners while itself suffering only 264 casualties.

Meanwhile, in the VI Corps' center, General Eagles' 45th Division "Thunderbirds"—including many Cherokee and Apache Indians—had an equally easy time. By 8:30 a.m. the division was able to report the situation on its three beaches: "First three waves landed. . . . Enemy resistance light." Most of the German troops hastily withdrew from Sainte-Maxime, once a fashionable resort town with pastel-painted hotels, but Thunderbird units still had to root out a handful of enemy soldiers who made a last-ditch stand in a concrete bunker with a 3-inch gun. A tank was called in to end the fight. At point-blank range of 50 yards, the tank scored two direct hits, blowing the bunker to bits along with its seven defenders.

The 45th Division Thunderbirds accomplished all of their assigned D-day missions and took 205 prisoners while suffering 109 casualties.

On the VI Corps' right, in the 36th Division's sector, things went well at first. The division seized two of its three beaches with little trouble, and General Dahlquist followed the troops ashore at 10 a.m. But the third assault, scheduled for the afternoon, ran into a snag.

This attack was aimed at the little port of Fréjus, which commanded not only the highway to Le Muy and the interior but also an excellent coastal road to Toulon and Marseilles. Fréjus was badly needed and, on the theory that it would be resolutely defended and might require special treatment, the attack there was not scheduled to take place until 2 o'clock in the afternoon.

As the assault was about to get under way, Generals Truscott and Patch watched with Admiral Hewitt from their command ship, the *Catoctin*. The landing craft circled several thousand yards offshore, while drone boats—remote-controlled vessels filled with high explosives to be detonated over underwater obstacles—headed toward the Fréjus beach. But the boats soon began to behave crazily (German radio operators were later credited with jamming the remote controls). Truscott saw one of them that "went out of control, dashed wildly up and down the beach, turned out

to sea to our consternation, then turned about again."

Intimidated by the berserk drone boats, the landing craft remained well offshore until 2:30, a half hour behind schedule. Then all the landing craft made an unplanned move. Recalled Truscott: "While we watched helplessly, to our profound astonishment the whole flotilla turned about and headed to sea again. Hewitt, Patch and I were furious."

The landing craft had been recalled by Rear Admiral Spencer Lewis, a veteran of the great Pacific sea battle at Midway. When the drones failed to breach the underwater obstacles off the Fréjus beach, Lewis tried to consult the 36th Division Commander, Dahlquist. But the general had gone ashore with the main force and was out of touch.

Admiral Lewis, unwilling to let the landing craft run the gauntlet of dangerous drones, decided to alter the Fréjus landing on his own responsibility. Instead, the men were immediately put ashore on an alternate beach nearby, and they moved to attack the port from the rear. When Dahlquist learned of the switch, he sent Lewis a message of thanks: "Appreciate your prompt action in changing plan. . . . Opposition irritating but not too tough so far." But Lewis' action, wrote Truscott, was "a grave error, which merited reprimand at least, and most certainly no congratulation. Except for the otherwise astounding success of the assault, it might have had even graver consequences."

An astounding success it had surely been, on the 36th Division's front as elsewhere; while suffering only 75 casualties, the 36th captured 236 prisoners on D-day and even took Fréjus without much trouble the next day. By then, the focal point of action had shifted to the west. For there, on D-plus-1, the French returned in force to their homeland.

"I kept my eyes closed so as not to be aware of too much happiness too soon." So said a French soldier of his homecoming. "And then I bent down and scooped up a handful of sand, with the feeling that what I was doing was a private act, separate from anybody else's." Many French soldiers had the same sense of exultation on touching the sand and soil of France. A witness to one French landing saw the troops "massed in the bows of the ship, fascinated by the beach; they jumped down with a single bound, bent down to pick up a handful of sand, then skipped like madmen to the nearest pine trees, where they regrouped, shaking each

Fighting in besieged Toulon, French soldiers turn a captured enemy field gun against the Germans. The eight-day struggle for the port, leading to the surrender of the Germans on August 28, 1944, was "really most extraordinary," said French Admiral André Lemonnier. "Some streets were deserted while others were crowded with civilian population who strolled by as if the battle were taking place kilometers away." Citizens often directed troops to strong points blocking the French advance.

other's hands, or embracing like brothers meeting again after a long absence."

As he had long since demonstrated, General de Lattre bowed to no man in his love for France. Yet of his own homecoming, the voluble commander reported only that at 11 p.m. in Saint-Tropez, "I reached the Hotel 'Latitude 43' where General Patch had set up his command." De Lattre had no time to indulge in patriotic reflections. The Allied plan called for his Army B—then consisting only of the II Corps and assorted smaller units, totaling about 16,000 men, but scheduled to be heavily reinforced by new landings day after day—to attack Toulon and Marseilles one after the other. Toulon was to be taken by September 4 and Marseilles 20 days later.

But de Lattre meant to do better than that, much better; on August 19 he asked Patch's permission to go after the two great ports simultaneously. "General Patch gave me a free hand," de Lattre wrote. "Then I suddenly saw the clear, grave eyes of the American commander soften. With hesitation that was full of shyness, he brought out his pocket-book and from it he took a flower with two stems, which was beginning to fade: 'Look,' he said, breaking it in two and handing me one of the stems; 'a young girl gave me it on the slopes of Vesuvius on the day before we embarked. She said it would bring me luck. Let us each keep half.' "

De Lattre set in motion a neat plan to encircle Toulon and attack the port from all sides. Brigadier General Charles Diego Brosset marched his veteran Free French 1st Infantry Division due west along the coastal highway and cordoned off Toulon from the east. Major General Aimé de Goislard de Monsabert led his Algerian 3rd Infantry Division through the mountain fortifications north of Toulon, then moved south to invest the city from the north and the west. Meanwhile, Allied naval forces closed in on the forts defending Toulon's southern approaches. On the 19th of August the honor of opening the bombardment was fittingly awarded to a French battleship, the *Lorraine*. De Lattre started his land assault the next day.

The German commander of Toulon, Rear Admiral Heinrich Ruhfus, had at his disposal some 25,000 men, about 100

light guns and 60 heavy ones, 30 forts and scores of pill-boxes and minefields. He also had an order from Hitler requiring him to hold the city "to the last cartridge." Ruhfus did his best, but it was not nearly enough. By August 22 Toulon was isolated and doomed.

The assault continued for a week and took several odd turns. A German-speaking French colonel tapped the telephone lines leading to Cap Brun Fort and told its commander that new orders from the Führer required him to shout "Heil Hitler" three times, blow up his guns and surrender the fort. The German officer obeyed to the letter. While the Free French 1st Division marked time on Toulon's outskirts, General Brosset found an undefended road, jumped into his jeep and entered the city alone. He returned jubilant. "Get a move on," he shouted to his troops. "I've already kissed at least 200 girls." Through it all, French forces continually pressed inward, squeezing the defenders into an ever-shrinking perimeter.

At 8 a.m. on August 28, Admiral Ruhfus appeared before General de Lattre to surrender Toulon. De Lattre gave him three hours to turn over detailed plans of all minefields in the area: "I warned him unequivocally that, after that interval, he would be shot if in his sector a single one of my men trod upon a German mine. Three hours later I had the plans." He also had 17,000 prisoners. The French had lost some 2,700 men killed or wounded.

Even as the assault on Toulon began on August 20, Colonel Léon Jean Chappuis and his 7th Infantry Regiment of the Algerian 3rd Division peeled off from the attack force and followed a French tank column west toward Marseilles. Waiting there apprehensively were Major General Hans Schaefer and 16,000 German troops, many of whom had wandered into the city after their units were routed on the invasion beaches to the east. An outer defense ring had been established in the city's sprawling suburbs, with massive roadblocks on all four of the main highways leading into Marseilles. Within the city, the defenses were anchored on redoubts in the port area to the north and on the heights of Notre-Dame de la Garde to the south. The defense system seemed impressive, but it was riddled with gaps that the French were soon to exploit.

When Chappuis arrived outside Marseilles on August 21, he learned that the Resistance had started an uprising in the city and that his troops were needed to aid the fighters, who were under heavy German pressure. Chappuis was enthusiastic about the idea of breaking into the city at once, before more troops arrived, and so reported to headquarters. De Lattre and Monsabert arrived there from Toulon on August 22 to look over the situation. The doughty Monsabert favored an immediate attack, but de Lattre dismissed the proposal. The Resistance could at times be a bother, de Lattre explained to Monsabert, and he had no intention of allowing his troops to be "contaminated by the disorder of a city in a state of insurrection."

Monsabert furiously protested, banging his fist on a table—to no avail. But when he told Chappuis of de Lattre's negative decision, he added with a sly smile: "Those are the orders. But should you have the opportunity. . . ."

By 5 o'clock the next morning, two battalions of Chappuis' regiment were on the outskirts of Marseilles, enjoying a breakfast of wine and fruit provided by a delirious citizenry at the Madeleine crossroad. Monsabert arrived and marched into the city with the troops. They tried to arrange the surrender of the German garrison, but the effort failed. Fighting erupted—and there they were: some 800 French soldiers in the midst of 16,000 Germans. The rest of Monsabert's division was withdrawn from Toulon and arrived posthaste to join the battle for Marseilles.

It was an incongruous, untidy battle. "In a few yards," de Lattre wrote, "one passed from the enthusiasm of a liberated boulevard into the solitude of a machine-gunned avenue. In a few turns of the track, a tank covered with flowers was either taken by the assault of pretty, smiling girls or fired at by an 88mm shell." At one intersection, a warning was posted: "Beware, there is firing from the church."

That church, the historic Notre-Dame de la Garde, and its commanding heights were the objective of an all-out assault launched on August 25 by two companies of Algerian infantry and a French tank troop. At 11:30 a.m. two Sherman tanks, the "Jourdain" and the "Jeanne d'Arc," neared the church steps. The "Jeanne d'Arc" was destroyed by shellfire. The "Jourdain" was crippled by a mine, but its wounded commander, a Sergeant Lolliot, clambered out of the tank and attached the tricolor of France to the church's railing. At 4:30 p.m., Notre-Dame de la Garde finally fell.

Wrecked piers in Marseilles, dynamited by the Germans before they surrendered, greeted the victorious French when they took over the port on the 28th of August, 1944. However, reconstruction here proved a much easier job than it was in Cherbourg harbor, and within one month facilities were available for docking and unloading 26 vessels at a time.

While the battle was raging within Marseilles, a fierce and tireless contingent of warriors—6,000 in all—trotted barefoot beside their heavily laden mules through the hills rimming the city. They were Goumiers, Berber tribesmen from the Atlas Mountains of Morocco. The Goumiers had almost been left behind; in Italy they had refused to travel without their beloved mules, which required special transports. Moreover, there was official concern about their "violent instincts, which it would be regrettable to let them satisfy in France." But de Lattre saw to it that his Goumiers came along, and now they were sealing off the routes by which Schaefer's troops might escape from Marseilles.

Surrounded and cut off, with his bastions crumbling before assaults by the reinforced French, Schaefer decided to surrender the city, along with 7,000 surviving troops, on August 28—the same day that Toulon fell. General de Lattre sent a proud message to de Gaulle: "Today, D-plus-13, in Army B's sector there is no German not dead or captive."

De Lattre had captured Toulon a week ahead of the schedule, and Marseilles had fallen to his forces nearly a month before the target date. But not even that swift performance matched the speed that Truscott had in mind for his VI Corps' campaign. "Every military leader," the general wrote, "dreams of the battle in which he can trap the enemy without any avenues or means of escape and in which his destruction can be assured." In order to cut off and obliterate all of the German forces in southwestern France, Truscott had to move as quickly as Patton's Third Army in its race eastward.

Soon after his remarkable success on the invasion beaches, Truscott had sketched out flexible plans for exploiting whatever possibilities lay ahead. He had also established a provisional armored group, called Task Force Butler after its commander, Brigadier General Fred W. Butler, whom Truscott called "one of the most fearless men I ever met." On August 17—D-plus-2—Butler received his marching orders: he would drive northwest to the Durance River, holding his task force ready to head either north to Grenoble or west to

Montélimar on the Rhone. As Task Force Butler raced north, Truscott and Patch chose between those two objectives on August 20, and Truscott sent an urgent message to Butler: "You will move at first light 21 August with all possible speed to Montélimar. Block enemy routes of withdrawal up the Rhone valley in that vicinity."

Truscott was, as he described his tactics, trying "to set the stage for a classic—a 'Cannae'—in which we would encircle the enemy against an impassable barrier or obstacle and destroy him." In the fulfillment of that purpose, Montélimar, hitherto known best to bonbon fanciers as the nougat capital of France, was the key. Just north of the town, National Highway 7 ran through a narrow defile—the Cruas Gorge—between the Rhone and a commanding ridge several miles long and 1,000 feet high. Butler was to plug this bottleneck in the Germans' main retreat route. He would be followed to Montélimar by Dahlquist and elements of the 36th Division, looping northwest from the right flank of the VI Corps. By seizing and holding the dominant ridge in strength, the two forces would pin the German Nineteenth Army in a trap, to be dismembered at leisure.

To carry out his Cannae, Truscott set several other forces in motion. The 45th Division moved north, splitting Provence and herding German remnants westward toward the Rhone Valley and Highway 7. The 3rd Division formed what Truscott's war log tersely called the "bottom of nutcracker," driving the Germans north up the Rhone into the trap at Montélimar. Since that division had previously been assigned to a blocking position north of Toulon and Marseilles, protecting de Lattre's II Corps during its attacks on those cities, Truscott first had to persuade Patch to release the 3rd Division for his push north. That bit of persuasion took Truscott until August 24.

While these movements were taking place, General Frederick's 1st Airborne Task Force faced east, protecting the VI Corps' right flank. The paratroopers carried out their guard duty with casual efficiency—and, as it turned out, with considerable enjoyment as well. A *Yank* staff correspondent reported: "they called it the 'Champagne Campaign,' this war in the Maritime Alps, because of the way the champagne flowed in the celebrations of the liberated people at Antibes and Cannes and Nice. . . . But when they went back into the mountains, to their foxholes on the terraced hillsides under the shelter of the olive trees, they returned to a full-fledged war."

Truscott's vanguard forces plunged north. Butler's tanks roared through the countryside at top speed, pausing only to refuel or to crush the small German garrisons they encountered. At some times and places the infantrymen did not march; they rushed ahead at what they called the "Truscott trot," a pace just slightly short of double time. Reinforcements from the south also moved along at a brisk clip, but they were hopelessly outdistanced; many a GI made the whole advance without hearing a single shot. It was said by experienced newsmen who reported the drive that Truscott was out-Pattoning Patton.

Truscott had not overemphasized how important speed was in his drive toward the Montélimar gap. For on August 16, Hitler had signed an order authorizing General Blaskowitz to withdraw his armies from southern France. With the exception of the forces then penned up in Toulon, Marseilles and ports along the southwest coast of France, all German troops west of the Rhone and south of the Loire would retreat northward. By August 23 the 11th Panzer Division, which had finally managed to cross the Rhone on jerry-built barges, was racing north, clearing the way to Montélimar, preparing to make a gallant stand to hold open the vital pass beyond.

Yet Truscott's race-horse advance was not trouble-free. As early as August 21 his war journal carried an ominous entry: "36th fouled up."

The 36th Division had exhausted the gasoline supply provided for the beach assault, and to get its stalled vehicles moving again, General Truscott on August 22 had been forced to give the outfit 10,000 gallons of gasoline taken from the 45th Division. But even then the 36th did not move as smartly as Truscott wanted it to. For that, he blamed General Dahlquist.

On the 22nd of August Truscott flew north to see Dahlquist at his last reported stopover, Aspres, in central Provence. He found that the General was out in the field but learned, "to my profound dismay," that elements of Dahlquist's division and also of the corps' artillery, which the general should have sent on ahead to Montélimar, were still in bivouac. Angered, Truscott left a note of stiff reprimand at Dahlquist's headquarters.

He was to become angrier yet. On August 24, after returning to his headquarters 15 miles north of Saint-Tropez, Truscott flew north once again to meet with Dahlquist, whose entire division had now reached the vital ridge line north of Montélimar. Truscott was informed by Dahlquist that "he had launched an attack to capture the ridge that morning and his troops were now on the northern end." Reassured, Truscott again headed south, only to learn from aerial reconnaissance reports that German troops were still moving into Montélimar and through the gap. "In spite of assurances," Truscott stated, "our block on Highway 7 was not effective."

On August 26, Truscott flew north yet again to confront Dahlquist, this time determined to make a radical move. "John," he said, "I have come here with the full intention of relieving you from your command. You have reported to me that you held the high ground north of Montélimar and that you had blocked Highway 7. You have not done so. You have failed to carry out my orders. You have just five minutes in which to convince me that you are not at fault."

Dahlquist said unhappily that his men had seized the wrong ridge—but the mistake had been rectified and the 36th Division was now in fact in position commanding Highway 7. Truscott was still dissatisfied, but he relented and left Dahlquist in command.

For the next two days, the VI Corps hammered the fleeing German Nineteenth Army, blasting tanks of the 11th Panzer Division, piling up destroyed trucks and guns. When de Lattre later passed through the area, he saw a terrible sight: "Over tens of kilometres there was nothing but an inextricable tangle of twisted steel frames and charred corpses—the apocalyptic cemetery of all the equipment of the Nineteenth Army, through which only bulldozers would be able to make a way."

But Dahlquist's delay had exacted a high cost. A large part of the Nineteenth Army had squeezed to safety through the gap held open by the 11th Panzer, which survived the

battering to fight again and again on the road to Germany. Moreover, most of Blaskowitz' other army, the First, had evacuated the Bordeaux area and was escaping well to the north of the VI Corps' advance. But the closing of the Montélimar gap, although belated, did come in time to seal the fate of the last Germans in southwestern France. The rear guard of the First Army had little choice but to surrender or to die in pointless battle. In fact, nearly 20,000 Germans eventually surrendered in a single group.

Thus the invasion of southern France reached its strategic conclusion at Montélimar. Symbolically, the operation may be said to have ended on September 11, 1944, when American soldiers of Patton's Third Army linked up with some of de Lattre's men in the town of Saulieu, 40 miles west of Dijon. On September 15, the Seventh Army was absorbed into Eisenhower's command. For General Truscott, whose driving leadership and daring were major factors in the success of the operation, the campaign brought a promotion to lieutenant general—a rank that resulted in his transfer from the fighting VI Corps to the command of an army. He wound up the War back in Italy as the commander of the U.S. Fifth Army.

The controversy surrounding Operation Anvil-Dragoon did not end. Churchill still believed that the forces involved could have struck a more telling blow in a drive north from Italy. But even Churchill conceded that the invasion had "brought important assistance to General Eisenhower."

That was faint praise. The invasion summed up all the Allies had learned about amphibious operations. The landing was almost textbook perfect, and the subsequent drive north was extraordinary, with the Seventh Army covering nearly 500 miles in just one month despite logistic problems. Southwestern France, almost one third of the nation, was thereby liberated in concert with the rapid advances being made in northern France. The ports captured in the invasion would inject into the war against Germany a total of 905,000 American soldiers and 4,100,000 tons of matériel. Churchill may have had reservations about the operation, but U.S. Chief of Staff Marshall had none. Anvil-Dragoon, he said, was "one of the most successful things we did."

THE PARISIANS MASTER WAR

In chilly November, 1943, Parisians huddle on a grill to take advantage of warm air rising from the subway. Fuel for home heating was rationed by the Germans.

"DESPERATE STRUGGLE FOR EXISTENCE"

Passing a pork store named "To the Royal Ham," a frustrated shopper grimaces after noticing an all-too-familiar sign: "Today, Nothing."

In June 1940, as the triumphant German Army neared Paris, more than two million citizens fled the city, leaving behind only 700,000. But the fugitives could not escape the conquerors, and as they drifted back in the following months, they found Paris transformed almost beyond recognition.

Motor vehicles had virtually disappeared from the city streets—except for autos and trucks used by the Germans. Paris was unheated and unlighted most of the time—except for districts with public buildings and German quarters. In the capital of haute cuisine, Parisians considered themselves lucky to dine on dishes they would have scorned in peacetime: heifer's udder, sheep's lungs, fricassee of alley cat. In the capital of haute couture, once-fashionable women improvised gloves from turkey skin and hats from wood shavings. Practically everything was in short supply—except the Germans' repressive measures.

"Everyday life," a Parisian wrote, "became a desperate struggle for existence," and conditions grew steadily worse. The Germans rationed and price-fixed essential items and issued coupons that theoretically permitted Parisians to buy enough to survive. The meat and bread rations were about half the normal consumption. The wine ration was set at about two quarts a week, which the average Parisian was used to consuming in four meals. The coal ration was as low as 50 kilos (110 pounds) per month per family—enough to heat a one-room apartment for five days. But by spring, 1941, most necessities were rarely available in adequate supply. Occupation troops had first call on all foodstuffs.

The Parisians suffered helplessly under the regimen of shortages; their protests were ignored, and they could not rebel against armed men. They made do without everyday necessities. "We have forgotten," noted one local writer, "what such things as rice, butter, soap, coffee, and eggs are like." The most galling aspect of the Occupation was that many of these items were not really scarce. Some shopkeepers had plenty of coffee, but they were obliged to post signs reading, "The coffee that we roast and grind is not for sale, it is for the exclusive use of the German troops."

Aspiring to makeshift elegance in footwear, a Parisienne puts the finishing touches on a pair of homemade shoes fashioned of raffia with cardboard soles.

Legs pumping, two men on a tandem bicycle run a ventilating system ordinarily powered by electricity.

DARKNESS FALLS ON THE "CITY OF LIGHT"

The Parisians, proud of the capital's fame as the "City of Light," resented Occupation policies that consigned them to darkness much of the time. The Germans confiscated most of the French coal supply for their own use, with the result that electricity for Paris was drastically reduced. Most sections of the city were put on a schedule of rotating blackouts.

While the power was cut off, businesses carried on as best they could. Some shopkeepers moved goods onto the sidewalks to trade in daylight. Several movie theaters kept their projectors running on current from generators powered by sturdy bicyclists. The Gaumont Palace, one of Paris' biggest theaters, calculated that four men, pedaling at the rate of 13 miles an hour for six hours, could produce enough electricity for two full-length features.

Faced with blackouts and the curfew, many families chose to spend the evenings in their living rooms under a single, flickering light bulb. They played cards, Monopoly, dominoes and mah-jongg, and at 9:15 every night they pressed their ears against radios to listen to the forbidden broadcasts of the BBC. Yet even these modest pleasures faded as the Germans' fuel supplies dwindled. Slowly but steadily the Occupation authorities extended the blackouts in Paris. By 1944 the current flowed through the city only one hour a day: between 11 p.m. and midnight.

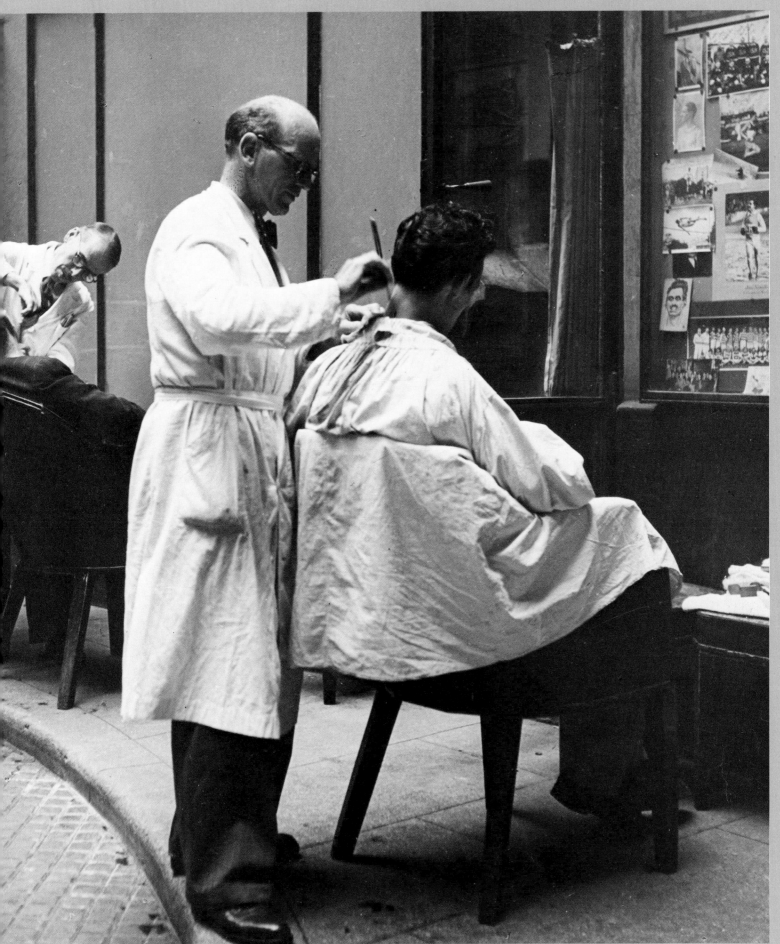

Undismayed by the usual power cutoff, two barbers and a manicurist take advantage of the daylight to groom their customers on a sunny sidewalk in Paris.

A Paris housewife stuffs paper into a makeshift stove that could boil a liter of water in 12 minutes.

LEARNING TO SURVIVE THE FUEL SHORTAGE

Thomas Kernan, an American who worked in occupied Paris before the United States entered the War, believed that "the hardships of the food shortage did not compare with the really terrible suffering caused by the fuel famine." Fuel for cooking was so scarce, he noted, that "a housewife could warm a dish on odd occasions only." Many women did heat small quantities of food with an ingenious device called *le réchaud papier*—the paper stove—that was fueled with scraps of paper *(left)* sprinkled with water for slow burning. There was a catch, though: paper was in short supply, too.

In the winter Parisians had to wear heavy outdoor clothing in their frigid apartments, and many, tired of shivering there, sought relief in the heated confines of post offices and subways. The museums and churches of Paris became as popular as the prewar cafés; there, said a newspaper article, the people "discovered a passion for archaeology, and a tireless devotion to some obscure saint, whose effigy was fanned by gentle blasts of warm air."

But the relief they were able to find was only temporary. "A hideous sight became gruesomely familiar in city streets," a Paris observer wrote. "Men and women, but especially children, blew fiercely at their hands in an effort to warm them. Their fingers were red and swollen. Unnatural bulges on them gaped with cracks or oozed pus from running sores."

"There comes a point," wrote Kernan, "where the human spirit can no longer withstand it." He cited the case of a housewife—"as patriotic as any"—who became so desperate that she asked the authorities to billet German officers in her home in a Paris suburb. "That was the only way she could get coal to heat the house, for no longer could she endure hearing her children crying from the cold."

Risking stiff fines to heat their frigid rooms, coal-less residents of Paris slip through the streets dragging branches that they cut illegally from the city's trees.

A bicycle-driven taxi slogs through the snow toward the Opera House in central Paris. This nearly empty square was often the scene of prewar traffic jams.

GETTING THERE IN SLOW MOTION

Day after day, the Parisians faced a stern battle just to get from their homes to jobs and stores across town. Frenchmen had to apply to the German authorities for permission to keep their cars, and those who received permits and gas rations generally found that gasoline pumps were dry.

Those who managed to keep their cars on the road ran them on a fuel produced by burning wood or charcoal in bolted-on devices called gasogenes.

Public transportation took up some of the slack. A record number of Parisians rode the subway, packed in shoulder to shoulder in second-class cars, while German troops traveled free in first class. Citizens who had relied on taxis paid high prices for rides in horse-drawn carriages

and *vélo-taxis*—two-wheeled carts driven by men pedaling bicycles. Parisians in a hurry might even catch an express *vélo-taxi* propelled by four veterans of the world's greatest bicycle race, the Tour de France.

But most Parisians—two out of three by 1944—depended on their own bicycles. "The entire city is pedaling 'round," wrote a newsman, "from nuns, going out to buy food or to make house-to-house collections, to respectable magistrates."

Using a specially rigged bicycle, a clever Parisian moves a bed across town.

A driver stokes his fuel converter; it powered his car by burning charcoal.

On their wedding day, a bride and groom start their honeymoon in a flower-bedecked coach fashioned from an automobile and towed by an old nag.

At a restaurant, hungry Parisians watch a chef as he serves the day's special, described on a chalkboard: croquette of horsemeat in mushroom and wine sauce, potatoes and vegetables. The bottom line of the sign reminds the customers that the serving is "ONE DISH . . . THAT'S ALL!"

Searching for edibles, two French women rummage through a pile of garbage in front of Les Halles, Paris' central market. On one occasion there was a minor riot at Les Halles. Women, queued up to purchase potatoes, clashed with German soldiers who requisitioned the supply.

CHRONIC HUNGER
IN THE CULINARY CAPITAL

Throughout the Occupation, the average Parisian lived on less than a third of his peacetime diet—and lost from five to 20 pounds. Moreover, he used up a good deal of his energy and time waiting in long lines for his meager fare.

It took the persistence and skills of a detective to find the makings of a square meal. People camped overnight outside of butcher stores rumored to have a meat delivery scheduled for the next morning. They bicycled far into the countryside to forage for fresh vegetables, eggs, meat and cheese. They also took to raising rabbits in bathtubs, poultry in rooftop coops and vegetables on the grounds of the Tuileries and the Luxembourg Gardens. Many sought out black marketeers who sold provisions at up to 20 times the price set by the Germans. A half pound of coffee, for example, was officially priced at 17 cents but sold for $2.75 on the black market.

Parisians bore up under their deprivations with bitter humor. According to one of their food-shortage jokes, their meat ration was so tiny that it could be wrapped in a subway ticket—if the stub had not been punched by the conductor. If the ticket had been punched, said the joke, the meat would fall through the hole.

5

As the Allies' massive seaborne invasion force was nearing the coast of southern France on August 14, 1944, events in northern France were about to take a dramatic turn of their own. There, as Allied ground troops tightened the noose around the German forces trapped in the Argentan-Falaise pocket, General Patton decided to pay a call on the U.S. XV Corps commander, General Haislip. At his headquarters south of Argentan, Haislip knew that the orders Patton was bringing with him would shape the future of the war in Europe and would determine the fate of Paris and its four million inhabitants.

The corps commander had reason to hope that these orders would conform to his wish for a swift, straight drive to liberate the French capital. Haislip spoke fluent French and had studied as a young officer at the Ecole de Guerre in Paris. He had under his command the only French division in Europe, the French 2nd Armored, and he felt keenly that Frenchmen must strike the ultimate symbolic blow for France by liberating Paris.

But Patton and the top Allied planners had more important objectives in mind. For the time being, Patton told Haislip, there would be no Allied effort to liberate the city. Two divisions of Haislip's XV Corps were to forge ahead only as far as Dreux, 45 miles from Paris, while the rest of the corps stayed at Argentan.

Haislip, bitterly disappointed, begged Patton to let the French 2nd Armored march on Paris. "George, you are wrong, you know," he said. "It will mean more to the French than anything else to think the only division they have in Europe is the first one to get into Paris and it will really jolly them up. It will thrill the whole country."

"Oh, to hell with that," replied Patton, unmoved. "We are fighting a war now."

In conveying the orders to Haislip, Patton was putting into effect the thinking of his superior, General Eisenhower. Ike was well aware of the immense spiritual uplift to the French—and to the whole Allied world—that would accompany the liberation of Paris. Yet his primary military objective clearly lay elsewhere: if his armies could thrust to the Rhine, now only 250 miles away, before the reeling Germans had time to regroup, the War might be ended in short order. But Eisenhower had another reason for not wanting to free the city. He knew that it would be a costly

A DIABOLICAL PLAN THWARTED

venture. Street fighting within a heavily defended Paris, a 24-page planning document from Allied Supreme Headquarters had warned, could result "in the destruction of the French capital." In addition, once taken, Paris would require "a civil affairs commitment equal to maintaining eight divisions in operation. . . . Paris food and medical requirements alone are 75,000 tons for the first two months, and an additional 1,500 tons of coal daily are likely to be needed for public utilities."

With the arrival of supplies still limited to the harbor at Cherbourg and the invasion beaches, Eisenhower already was operating on a logistical shoestring; even now, he was stripping incoming divisions of jeeps and trucks intended for battlefield use and assigning them to supply convoys. The round trip between Cherbourg and Paris was more than 400 miles, and each supply convoy would consume hundreds of gallons of gasoline at a time when, as Eisenhower would later recall, "I hurt every time I had to give up a gallon." His American field commander, General Bradley, put it another way: "If Paris could pull in its belt and live with the Germans a little longer, each 4,000 tons we saved would mean gasoline enough for a three days' motor march toward the German border."

The Allied plan was to go all out toward Germany. In the process, two arms—Montgomery's Twenty-first Army Group to the north and Bradley's Twelfth Army Group to the south—would be thrown around Paris, embracing the great city without storming it. The timetable called for the liberation of the city no earlier than the middle of September. But the plans for Paris were destined to be overwhelmed by events. Conspiring to upset the timetable were the urgent and inexorable will of the French to rule again in their capital, a contest between Communists and Gaullists for power in the city, the determination of Adolf Hitler to leave the French capital in ruins and, not least, the reluctance of a German general to become known to history as the man who destroyed Paris.

While the Allied leaders were debating what to do about Paris, the citizens of the great city were suffering from a variety of shortages and inconveniences. They were in dire need of food, electricity, municipal transport—and perhaps most of all, a renewal of their self-respect. In addition to the brutality of the German Occupation, the Parisians had endured hundreds of grating indignities. Each day, 250 elite German troops behind a brass band blaring "Preussens Glorie" ("Prussia's Glory") paraded down the Champs-Elysées from the Arc de Triomphe to the Place de la Concorde. The swastika flapped from the top of the city's most visible landmark, the Eiffel Tower, while the banned French tricolor could be viewed publicly in only one spot, a glass case in the Army Museum of Les Invalides.

The most potent and persistent force for a quick liberation of Paris was Charles de Gaulle. From his headquarters in Algeria, de Gaulle headed the French Committee of National Liberation, the central organization guiding the Free French war effort and coordinating the coalition of Communist, Gaullist and other anti-German guerrillas in France known as the Resistance. However, de Gaulle was far from being established as the unquestioned leader of France. He had formidable rivals in the Resistance—primarily Communists—who had the advantage of jockeying for position from within the country. In addition, many Allied officials considered him a pest, and even to his beleaguered countrymen he was little more than a voice from beyond, known to them by his BBC broadcasts.

De Gaulle realized that in order to become the acknowledged leader of liberated France, he would have to be recognized as the liberator of Paris. He understood, too, that if the city's civilian population, spurred by strident Communist factions in the Resistance, were to rise up and expel the Germans before he got to Paris, "on my arrival they would bind my brows with laurel, invite me to assume the place they would assign me, and thenceforth pull all the strings themselves."

Against that gloomy prospect, de Gaulle had been preparing for the assumption of power with painstaking care and consummate skill. His chances improved greatly on December 30, 1943, when Eisenhower visited Algiers and met with him for the first time. Near the end of the session, Ike said, "You were originally described to me in an unfavorable sense. Today, I realize that that judgment was wrong." "Splendid!" replied de Gaulle. "You are a man! For you know how to say, 'I was wrong!'" De Gaulle then went on to say to Ike: "It must be French troops that take possession of the capital." He meant forces under his own control as head of the French Committee of National Liberation. Eisenhower agreed.

In July of 1944, de Gaulle had taken another step toward becoming the undisputed leader of France. He traveled to Washington, D.C., to confer with President Roosevelt, who formally recognized him as the leader of a de facto French government sanctioned by the Allies to rule in liberated territory.

Now, in August 1944, as the Allied troops swept eastward across France, teams of Gaullist administrators, police, supply officers and even a traveling court-martial board followed close behind them, taking control of local governments in the name of the French Committee of National Liberation and Charles de Gaulle. These auxiliaries were under stern and specific orders to prevent Communist-dominated Resistance committees from gaining control of the newly liberated French cities and towns.

To de Gaulle the French Communists at this transitional stage of the war represented at least as fearsome a menace as the Germans. They were particularly powerful in the Paris Resistance, where they had an estimated 25,000 fighters under arms. To prevent a take-over by Communist factions in the city, de Gaulle methodically infiltrated his own representatives into the Paris Resistance. Among these was the 29-year-old General Jacques Chaban-Delmas, de Gaulle's top military man in Paris.

Chaban-Delmas had not the slightest doubt about the nature of the Leftist threat. "Whatever the cost," he later said, "the Communists would launch their insurrection, even if the result was the destruction of the most beautiful city in the world." He was right. The Communists, determined to challenge the Gaullists for power in Paris every step of the way, were convinced that their political advantage lay in fomenting rebellion in the city. If the uprising succeeded—and they believed it would—they could ride the wave of popular acclaim in France and deny de Gaulle the power he coveted.

Roger Villon, the Communist chief of staff of the Paris Resistance, was resolute in his belief that de Gaulle should not "march into Paris at the head of a conquering army and find the city gratefully prostrated at his feet." Villon was egged on by the commander of Communist military forces in Paris—Colonel Rol. Born Henri Tanguy, he had

served in the Spanish Civil War (and taken his *nom de guerre* from a comrade killed in that conflict). Rol was a dedicated party member whose courage and devotion to the cause were acknowledged even by his enemies. Like his Gaullist opposite number, Chaban-Delmas, Rol realized the importance of the prize now involved. "Paris," he said, "is worth 200,000 dead."

In his headquarters in East Prussia, Hitler was determined to reduce Paris to such a shambles that neither the Gaullists nor the Communists would stand to gain from its liberation. To carry out his plans, Hitler summoned to Rastenburg in the early part of August an officer from the Western Front who, in the words of an OKW superior, had "never questioned an order, no matter how harsh it was." Physically, Major General Dietrich von Choltitz hardly fit the autocratic Prussian stereotype. He was a pudgy little man, and although his face, as described by a colleague, was "as expressionless as the fat Buddha's," he possessed a certain burgomaster jollity.

But Choltitz' reputation as a wrecker of cities was fearsome. In May 1940, as a lieutenant colonel, he had ordered the heart of Rotterdam bombed to rubble, leaving 718 Dutch dead and 78,000 wounded or homeless. The siege of Sebastopol in the Crimea, where he won general's rank, left him with an arm wound and only 347 able-bodied men out

Portly Major General Dietrich von Choltitz, the German commander of Paris, vowed to "personally shoot down in my own office the next man who comes to me suggesting we abandon Paris without a fight." But the defense he set up outside the city was soon overcome by the advancing French 2nd Armored Division.

of the original 4,800 in his regiment; but he took the city, and demolished it. And during the retreat from Russia, Choltitz covered the German rear, leaving behind only scorched earth. Such was his notoriety that he was widely blamed for the August 1944 destruction of Warsaw, where more than 100,000 died; in fact, he had been on the Western Front at the time. Choltitz was keenly—and ruefully—aware of his infamy. "It is always my lot," he said, "to defend the rear of the German army. And each time it happens I am ordered to destroy each city as I leave it."

In recent days, Choltitz had been greatly distressed by Germany's continuing defeats and had felt much in need of a boost to his flagging faith and spirit. As he arrived at Hitler's headquarters, he felt sure the Führer could provide the uplift he needed. What he encountered instead was one of the most bizarre and unsettling experiences of his life.

Hitler, still shaken by the July 20 assassination attempt, launched into a tirade shortly after greeting Choltitz. "Since the 20th of July, Herr General," he cried, "dozens of generals—yes, dozens—have bounced at the end of a rope because they wanted to prevent me, Adolf Hitler, from continuing my work."

Choltitz was aghast. "He was in a state of feverish excitement," he later said. "Saliva was literally running from his mouth. He was trembling all over and the desk on which he was leaning shook with him. He was bathed in perspiration and became more agitated."

Hitler came to the point. "Now," he said to Choltitz, "you're going to Paris." The city "must be utterly destroyed. On the departure of the Wehrmacht, nothing must be left standing, no church, no artistic monument." Even the water supply would be cut off, so that—in the Führer's words—"the ruined city may be a prey to epidemics."

Choltitz later recalled Hitler's harangue with dismay. "I was convinced there and then," he said, that "the man opposite me was mad!" His confidence in Hitler shattered, Choltitz left the meeting more despondent than ever—and, perhaps for the first time in his military career, questioning his own resolve to carry out an order.

Soon afterward, he paid a visit to Field Marshal von Kluge, commander of Army Group B, just six days before Kluge committed suicide. "I'm afraid, my dear Choltitz," said Kluge at the end of the meeting, "Paris may become a rather disagreeable assignment for you. It has the air of a burial place about it." Choltitz' reply was full of grim sarcasm. "At least," he said, "it will be a first class burial."

In Paris, Choltitz set up his headquarters in the elegant Hôtel Meurice, near the Place de la Concorde. From his bedroom window he could look down on the lush treetops of the Tuileries. There, in the days that followed, the stout German spent long hours in lonely contemplation of his dilemma. He was haunted by the thought that the man to whom he had sworn blind obedience was mad and that his country's cause was lost. As a patriotic German soldier, he was prepared to defend Paris against the advancing Allies; but, sensitive to the city's beauty and traditions, he was loath to destroy it. To disobey Hitler's orders would endanger his own life and the lives of his wife and children in Germany. Yet he knew that if he carried out the Führer's directives, history would damn him as the man who destroyed one of the world's most glorious cities.

As he pondered his problem, Choltitz was confronted with a situation that was to directly affect his decision: unrest in the city's police force. The gendarmes had long been caught in a cruel dilemma of their own, despised by the Parisians for carrying out the harsh Occupation orders of the Germans, yet distrusted by the Occupation authorities. As one of his first acts as commander of Paris, Choltitz set about disarming the police. In retaliation, the police made it clear that the Germans had good reasons for concern. A Resistance group within the police department called a strike for August 15, grimly warning: "Police who do not obey this order to strike will be considered traitors and collaborators." The strike was highly effective: only a handful of the gendarmes manned their posts. Events were now moving at such a pace as to force Choltitz' hand.

On the gray, damp Saturday morning of August 19, Amedée Bussière, the head prefect of the Paris police, awakened to the sound of a throng gathered outside the bedroom of his apartment at the Prefecture, the police headquarters on the Ile de la Cité opposite Notre-Dame. He hoped that his men were returning to duty, but he was mistaken. In the courtyard below, a slender blond man in a checked suit was addressing the crowd. As a trumpet sounded and voices lifted in the long-forbidden "Marseillaise," Yves Bayet, head of the Gaullist police faction in the Paris Police Committee of Liberation, proclaimed: "In the name of the Republic and Charles de Gaulle, I take possession of the Prefecture of Police."

On the previous day, the call for an uprising—including seizure of the Prefecture—had gone out from Communist Resistance leaders, who had hoped to keep the Gaullists ignorant of the plan until it was too late to do anything about it. But Alexandre Parodi, de Gaulle's top political representative in Paris, got word from an informer planted among the Communists—and Parodi, forewarned, struck first at the Prefecture. Ironically, this first major act of insurrection was led by the Gaullists—who, on orders from de Gaulle himself, had fiercely opposed open rebellion. But Gaullist leaders in Paris felt compelled to preempt the plans of their archrivals for power, the Communists. For their part, the Communists, hearing that they had been beaten to the punch at the Prefecture, immediately embarked on their plan to ambush German soldiers and vehicles all over Paris. Soon sharp gunfights could be heard across the city, as well-organized Resistance bands—Communist and Gaullist alike—began seizing police substations, post offices and government buildings. By nightfall, both sides had suffered heavy casualties; the Germans alone lost more than 50 killed and 100 wounded.

Late that night, Choltitz stood on the balcony of his hotel room, watching a girl in a red dress as she rode her bicycle through the Tuileries toward the Place de la Concorde. With Choltitz was Raoul Nordling, for 18 years the Swedish consul general in Paris and the managing director of the SKF factories, which made ball bearings that had helped keep the German war machine rolling. Choltitz, angered by the uprising in Paris, was nevertheless in a pensive mood. "I like those pretty Parisiennes," he said. "It would be a tragedy to have to kill them and destroy their city."

To Nordling, the destruction of Paris was unthinkable. He felt he owed much to the city in which he had spent his entire adult life—and that he deeply loved. He had already begun to pay that debt: during the week he had successfully negotiated with Choltitz for the release of more than 4,000 French political prisoners. With all his eloquence, Nordling now argued for the salvation of Paris.

"I am a soldier," Choltitz said. "I get orders. I execute them." From the area around the Resistance-held Prefecture came a spatter of gunfire. "I'll get them out of their Prefecture," Choltitz vowed. "I'll bomb them out of it."

"Do you realize," Nordling asked, "your near misses will fall on Notre-Dame and the Sainte-Chapelle?"

That could not be helped, Choltitz replied to Nordling. "You know the situation. Put yourself in my place. What alternative do I have?"

Nordling answered the plaintive question immediately. He proposed a cease-fire "to pick up the dead and wounded" of the spreading insurrection; if the cease-fire was successful, it might be turned into a full-fledged truce. The idea appealed to Choltitz: a truce would release troops, now tied down in the attempt to quell the uprising, to man the defense line Choltitz was setting up around Paris.

Two hours after his meeting with Nordling, as he considered the proposed truce, Choltitz received an order from Hitler instructing him to prepare the Seine bridges for destruction. "Paris," the Führer declared, "must not fall into the hands of the enemy except as a field of ruins."

Choltitz, a hard-bitten soldier for 29 of his 49 years, now faced his most agonizing decision. As an experienced tactician, he knew that Hitler's order could not halt the Allied advance. The Americans were already across the river north and south of the city. "What military value could the destruction of the bridges possibly have in this situation?" Choltitz later wrote. "Even if only three of the 60 bridges were to remain intact, the entire action would prove militarily worthless. . . . Additionally, I myself needed the bridges for troop movements within the city."

Beyond the military considerations, Choltitz found himself being influenced by more basic human emotions. "In what state of mind could I, without necessity, destroy this city, which had endured, calmly and wisely, though grudgingly, for four years under German occupation?" he asked himself. "It had been my firm commitment from the very beginning as a decent soldier to protect the civilian population and their magnificent city to the greatest extent possible." Weighing all of the factors that had pressed so heavily on him since his arrival in Paris, Choltitz made up his mind: he would accept a cease-fire.

Acting as an intermediary, Nordling outlined the terms of

his proposed cease-fire to Gaullist contacts he had cultivated in the Paris Resistance during the Occupation. Then, at a hastily convened early-morning meeting, Chaban-Delmas and his Gaullist associates presented the truce to Resistance leaders. Unfortunately for the Communists, who wanted to continue the fight, the deck was stacked against them. With communications difficult in the city and with events surging ahead at a tremendous clip, only one of their leaders—Roger Villon—was informed of the meeting; in fact, only six of the 16 Resistance chiefs eligible to vote were present.

Villon spoke out against the cease-fire. "The people of Paris have risen and are ready to liberate the capital themselves," he said. "To make them lay down their arms would be to curb their spirit and balk them of their victory." But the prevailing sentiment in the meeting was against Villon. The Germans were still too strong to be defeated, said the Gaullists, and Choltitz might destroy the city. The cease-fire proposal passed five to one.

Under the terms of the truce, Choltitz agreed to recognize members of the FFI, the coalition of Gaullist, Communist and other underground Resistance fighters, as regular troops and to treat them as prisoners of war if captured, instead of executing them as terrorist guerrillas. The Germans also accepted the FFI occupation of public buildings already seized (these by now included the Hôtel de Ville, which housed the municipal government and had been taken over by the Communist factions in the Resistance in response to the Gaullist occupation of the Prefecture). The FFI, for its part, agreed not to attack German-held strongholds and to allow German troop movements along several major arteries.

Little by little, as word of the cease-fire spread across the city, the firing stopped. A curtain of silence descended on the buildings whose courtyards, hallways and staircases had echoed during the day with gunfire. The FFI set up mobile kitchens, where exhausted Resistance fighters were given a snack, some hot coffee and two packs of cigarettes each.

But the truce quickly began to crumble. Colonel Rol, the Communist military leader, furious at the agreement that had been concluded without his consent a few hours before, feverishly began to undermine it, hoping ultimately to gain control in Paris. "The order is insurrection," Rol told his followers. "As long as there is a single German left in the streets of Paris, we shall fight."

Slowly but steadily throughout the day, along sweeping boulevards and in dark alleys, the uprising regained its lost momentum; four truckloads of German soldiers were ambushed and doused with Molotov cocktails, which sent the burned occupants screaming through the narrow streets. Fearful of German retribution, Gaullists sought desperately to stop the shooting. "Rol and the men around him are leading Paris to a massacre!" cried Chaban-Delmas. But Rol held fast, and the rebellion spread.

At the Hôtel Meurice, Choltitz' glum contemplation of the truce breakdown was interrupted by a telephone call. At the other end of the line was General Jodl, Hitler's operations chief, wanting to know how much progress Choltitz had made in executing Hitler's order to destroy the city. In fact, Choltitz had done little. He tried to excuse the delay by claiming that his troops had been totally occupied with quelling the insurrection. This was the first indication Jodl (or through him, Hitler) had of the extent of the Paris uprising. For a few moments he seemed dumbstruck. Then, speaking deliberately but with a noticeable edge to his voice, Jodl concluded the conversation: "Whatever happens, the Führer expects you to carry out the widest destruction possible in the area assigned to your command."

The news from Paris, which jolted Hitler and Jodl, disturbed Eisenhower as well. When he first heard that the Resistance was fighting in the city, Ike was—he later said—

Wearing American combat gear, members of the French 2nd Armored Division fire rifles and a bazooka at German forces fighting a delaying action at Châteaufort, eight miles southwest of Paris, on August 24, 1944. To enable the Free French to put a modern army in the field, the United States provided about 3.25 million tons of equipment, including more than 1,400 tanks and almost 50.2 million small arms.

"damned mad." It was "just the kind of situation I didn't want, a situation that wasn't under our control, that might force us to change our plans before we were ready for it." Because of the fighting, he faced the dismal prospect of a meeting with de Gaulle, whom he quite rightly suspected of intending to try "to get us to change our plans to accommodate his political needs."

After a precarious flight from Algiers (his plane got lost in fog over the English Channel while trying to link up with a British fighter escort), de Gaulle landed at Cherbourg; his plane had fuel for only two more minutes of flying. Promptly informed of the uprising in Paris, he sprang into action. He flew off in his refueled plane to present his case to Eisenhower at Ike's forward headquarters not far away.

When the two men met, Eisenhower explained to de Gaulle how he planned to pinch off Paris and let it hang there for later plucking. According to Eisenhower, de Gaulle "immediately asked us to reconsider on Paris. He made no bones about it; he said there was a serious menace from the Communists in the city." To Eisenhower, this was a political argument, running counter to strategy—and he found it unacceptable.

Ike suspected that the Germans were reinforcing Paris, and "we might get ourselves in a helluva fight there." But de Gaulle insisted that the prompt liberation of Paris was of paramount importance, and he backed his plea with a threat. He was ready if necessary, he said, to remove Major General Jacques Leclerc's French 2nd Armored Division, now temporarily attached to the American V Corps under Major General Leonard Gerow, from the Allied command and send it to Paris on his own authority. Eisenhower merely smiled—serene in his belief that the 2nd Armored was so dependent on American equipment and supplies that it "couldn't have moved a mile if I didn't want it to."

De Gaulle had been rebuffed, but he was far from defeated. Departing, he turned to an aide and asked: "Where is General Leclerc?"

At that moment, and throughout the next nerve-fraying day of Monday, August 21, General Leclerc was at Argentan, more than 100 miles from Paris. There, as de Gaulle later wrote, the 2nd Armored Division was being kept under "close supervision of General Gerow . . . as if someone

feared it might make off toward the Eiffel Tower." In fact, Leclerc was straining to do just that. He was an impetuous man, who had been waiting for four years for such an opportunity. His real name was not Leclerc but Jacques-Philippe de Hautecloque. He had taken the pseudonym to protect the family he had left behind in Occupied France. In July 1940, some three weeks after France's surrender, he had bicycled across the Pyrenees and into Spain; from there he had traveled to London to join de Gaulle. His first command, in French Equatorial Africa, had consisted of three officers, two missionaries, seven farmers and five civil servants, equipped with a single dugout canoe. Now, on August 21, 1944, he commanded 16,000 men with 2,000 vehicles—and he was eagerly awaiting the signal to lead his countrymen back into Paris.

As it happened, Eisenhower had miscalculated in assuming that Leclerc's division was unable to move without American help. In recent days, the French regiments had deliberately failed to report their vehicle losses so that their gasoline ration would not be cut. They also continued to requisition fuel and ammunition for vehicles and weapons that had been lost in the fighting around the Argentan-Falaise pocket. In nighttime forays, moreover, men of the French 2nd Armored had taken additional supplies from Allied dumps. By this unorthodox means, Leclerc had squirreled away enough gasoline and ammunition to get his division to Paris.

Yet, as a professional soldier, Leclerc still respected what he called the "rules of military subordination," and at least for the moment, he was willing to settle for a token advance on Paris. In strict secrecy, Leclerc ordered Lieut. Colonel Jacques de Guillebon, at the head of a force of about 150 men in tanks, armored cars and personnel carriers, to reconnoiter the routes toward—and, if the opportunity arose, into—Paris. As General Bradley later related it, Gerow himself first spotted the wayward column after it had passed through Chartres. "And just where in hell do you think you're going?" Gerow asked a French captain. The reply, accompanied by a smile and a shrug: "To Paris—yes?" The V Corps commander was outraged at such blatant insubordination. He halted the armored column in its tracks and sent it back to Argentan.

While Leclerc had been scouting the possibilities for a

march into Paris, radical Resistance forces inside the city were urging the populace to greater action. Three new Resistance newspapers—*Le Parisien Libéré, Défense de la France* and *Libération*—appeared in the capital on August 21. Each of the papers, sired by the Communist forces of Colonel Rol, carried the huge headline, *Aux Barricades!*—the stirring battle cry that had echoed throughout Paris' revolution-filled past.

Despite danger to themselves and to their beloved city, Parisians within the next two days would answer that call by building more than 400 barricades. People of all ages tore up paving stones, felled trees, ripped up railings, turned over cars and trucks, then piled the debris in boulevards and alleyways to hamper German movement. In Saint Germain des Prés, on the corner of the Rue St. Jacques, battered pictures of Hitler and other Nazi leaders were hung on the barricades in exposed positions where attacking Germans would have to fire on them. "Hour by hour, methodically, the barricades close in round the Germans like a trap," wrote an observer. "Patiently, cunningly, with all the vast fury of insurgent Paris, the spider's web is woven."

As the street fighting flared, the Resistance made steady gains. Dozens of key buildings—newspaper offices, government headquarters and Elysée Palace, home of French heads of state—fell into FFI hands. At the Bank of France, the tricolor hung from the façade, while Resistance fighters divvied up a treasure stored inside that was more prized than money in luxury-starved Paris—400,000 bottles of cognac, three million cigars and 235 tons of sugar.

Meanwhile, at a violent conclave of factional leaders, top Resistance chiefs debated whether to try to restore the shattered cease-fire. An angry voice denounced the truce with Choltitz: "You don't make gentlemen's agreements with murderers!" Chaban-Delmas, the Gaullist general, furiously retorted: "You want to massacre 150,000 people for nothing!" Declared Roger Villon, the Communist political leader: "I've never seen such a gutless French general." And then, playing his trump card, Villon vowed that if the truce were restored, the Communists would "plaster every wall in Paris with a poster accusing the Gaullists of stabbing the people of Paris in the back." Alexandre Parodi, the Gaullist political chief, gave in. "My God," he said. "They're going to destroy Paris now. Our beautiful Notre-Dame will be bombed to ruins." But Villon was unmoved. "So what if Paris is destroyed?" he said. "We will be destroyed along with it. Better Paris be destroyed like Warsaw than that she live another 1940."

Fortunately for Paris, however, the fate of the city rested in the hands of Choltitz. He had chosen to ignore—as long as he could—Hitler's order to immolate the city. Anticipating reprisal from the Führer, he said to an aide: "I will sit on the last bridge and blow myself up along with it because it will be the only thing left for me."

As the violence spread, Choltitz made a desperate gesture to calm the rampaging French patriots. Food supplies were dwindling, and he offered to turn some meat over to the Resistance. When the Frenchmen proudly refused to take it from German hands, a face-saving compromise was arranged and the meat was sent to Nordling, who then gave it to the Resistance. But the offering had little effect: the fighting had taken on an irresistible momentum.

Choltitz decided to meet with Nordling and try another tack. As the two men faced each other across a decanter of whiskey in the German commander's headquarters at the Hôtel Meurice, Choltitz said wryly: "Your truce, Herr Consul General, doesn't seem to be working very well." Nordling agreed and commented that perhaps the only man who could calm Paris, Charles de Gaulle, was elsewhere. In matter-of-fact tones, Choltitz asked a wholly unanticipated question: "Why doesn't someone go to see him?"

In his many years as a diplomat, Nordling had rarely been so astonished. Hesitating, groping for the explicit meaning of the question, he asked if Choltitz would authorize someone to pass through the German lines to seek out the Allied command.

"Why not?" asked Choltitz.

Taking a sheet of paper from his jacket, Choltitz explained that it contained the formal orders for Paris' demolition. So far, he said, he had managed to resist the orders, but time was running out. Only the presence in Paris of Allied troops could prevent the debacle. "You must realize," he said, "that my behavior in telling you this could be interpreted as treason." He paused, then added: "Because what I am really doing is asking the Allies to help me."

When Nordling, as a neutral diplomat, volunteered to

approach the Allies, Choltitz quickly wrote a pass to enable him to get out of the city and make contact with the Allied command and, ultimately, with de Gaulle: "The Commanding General of Greater Paris authorizes the Consul General of Sweden R. Nordling to leave Paris and its line of defense." Then, ushering Nordling out of his office, Choltitz offered a farewell admonition. "Go fast," he said. "Twenty-four, forty-eight hours are all you have."

As Nordling was leaving the German headquarters, he was struck by a troubling thought: perhaps de Gaulle and the Allied commanders would view him less as the well-meaning Swedish consul general than as the purveyor of SKF ball bearings to Germany. To clear the way for his mission, he decided to take with him two men with strong Gaullist connections: Alexandre de Saint-Phalle, treasurer of the Resistance in Paris, and Jean Laurent, who in 1940 had served with de Gaulle in the Ministry of Defense.

Added to the party on Choltitz' advice was Emil "Bobby" Bender, ostensibly the representative of a Swiss paper-pulp company but actually an agent of Abwehr, the German intelligence arm, whose status could be counted on to shepherd the party past security checkpoints. Since 1940, Bender had been a familiar figure in Paris nightclubs; now, to protect himself or from real affection for Paris, he agreed to help save the city (he had already helped Nordling arrange for the release of French political prisoners).

A fifth member joined the group; he called himself "Arnoux" and claimed to be a Red Cross representative. He was, in fact, Colonel Claude Ollivier, head of the British intelligence service in France. Finally, self-invited, was an Austrian nobleman, Baron Erich Posch-Pastor von Camperfeld, who had opposed the Nazis, been interned at Dachau, later escaped to France and joined the Resistance.

That afternoon came a near-fatal hitch in the plan. As he was getting ready to leave, 62-year-old Raoul Nordling slumped to the floor of the Swedish consulate with a heart attack, which, though it proved to be mild, nonetheless precluded any possibility of his leading the mission. Hastily picked to replace him was the one other man in the city whose initials and last name matched those on the Choltitz pass: Raoul Nordling's brother Rolf.

And so the oddly assorted group finally set out—five men in Nordling's car and Bobby Bender in his speedy little Citroën—only to be stopped near the village of Trappes by a German soldier, clad for comfort in the August heat in a polka-dot bathing suit but wearing his helmet and brandishing a submachine gun. At that point, Bender made up for any past sins he may have committed: shouting angrily, he showed his Abwehr papers, along with the Choltitz pass, to an SS captain who had come to investigate. The captain rejected them. "I don't give a damn what general signed it," he said of the pass. "Since the 20th of July, we don't obey Wehrmacht generals." Furious, Bender demanded that the officer call Choltitz' headquarters for orders. Minutes later, Rolf Nordling and his group were on their way.

But they were unable to make contact with the Allied command until the next morning. By that time, Leclerc's tanks were already rolling toward Paris, spurred by an entirely separate two-man mission that had set forth from the beleaguered capital to seek arms from the Allies and had changed its purpose en route.

Major Roger Gallois was Colonel Rol's chief of staff. Two days earlier, Rol, whose insurrection required more weapons to fill willing but empty hands, had jumped at an offer from Dr. Robert Monod, who led a double life as the official health inspector for the Paris area and medical chief for the Resistance. Monod agreed to guide a Rol emissary through the German lines to "establish a liaison with the Allies and ask for arms." Rol chose Gallois for the job.

Gallois and Monod traveled only 18 miles that first day and night before stopping to rest in the village of Saint-Nom-la-Breteche. The two were longtime friends, and as they talked by candlelight, Monod, an anti-Communist especially resentful of Communists planted in his own office, urged Gallois not to help Rol grasp control of Paris by insurrection. Instead, the doctor said, Gallois should try to get the Allies to go to Paris as quickly as possible, so the city would be saved from destruction by the Germans. Gallois listened carefully. "Robert," he said finally, "I think you're right." With those words, Gallois changed goals: instead of seeking arms for Colonel Rol, he would try to convince Allied commanders that they, and not the insurrectionists, must accomplish the liberation of Paris.

The next day, Gallois came upon an American soldier, eating canned rations by the side of the road. "I come from

Paris," Gallois dramatically declared, "with a message for General Eisenhower!"

"Yeah?" said the American. "So what?"

Despite that massive display of disinterest, Gallois was placed in a jeep and taken to the headquarters of General Patton, whose Third Army had crossed the Seine that same day. When he had first heard of the Paris uprising, Patton had been less than sympathetic: "They started their goddamned insurrection. Now let them finish it." Aroused from sleep, he was hardly in better humor. "Okay," he told the disheveled French Resistance officer. "I'm listening. What's your story?" And when Gallois finished talking, Patton flatly turned down his plea: the Resistance would have to "accept the consequences" of its own insurrection, he said.

Still, Gallois must have impressed Patton; at any rate, he was soon on his way by jeep to General Bradley's headquarters at Laval, where he arrived on the morning of August 22.

There, Brigadier General Edwin L. Sibert, Bradley's intelligence officer, who had been alerted by Patton's headquarters, was waiting impatiently to meet with Gallois and to get a firsthand account of the situation in Paris. Sibert had delayed a flight with Bradley to Eisenhower's new headquarters at Grandchamp, just outside Falaise, where he was to attend a conference with the Supreme Commander. Gal-

lois, his failure to convince Patton still rankling, passionately poured out his fears for the preservation of Paris and the survival of its populace. "The people of Paris want to liberate their capital themselves and present it to the Allies," he said. "But they cannot finish what they have started. You must come to our help or there is going to be a terrible slaughter."

Sibert was silent. But as he gathered his papers before leaving, he confided some information to Gallois that gave cause for hope. "Your impatient lion, Leclerc, is coming today," he said, knowing that the French general was later to meet with Bradley. "We may have some news for him tonight." Sibert had one other piece of news that he did not share with Gallois: Eisenhower was wavering about Paris.

It had become increasingly evident to Ike that the French capital was in real peril. Just as Choltitz dreaded being known to history as the man who destroyed Paris, Eisenhower had no wish to be responsible for contributing to the city's ruin by doing nothing to save it. Beyond that, Ike was having second thoughts about the military considerations, thoughts he expressed that morning in a cable to his superior in Washington, U.S. Army Chief of Staff Marshall. He acknowledged the fact that Paris' supply needs made it desirable to delay its liberation, but, he added, "I do not believe this is possible. If the enemy tries to hold Paris with any real strength, he would be a constant menace to our flank. If he largely concedes the place, it falls into our hands whether we like it or not."

Finally, there was the matter of de Gaulle, about whom Ike's feelings were ambivalent. Eisenhower was often annoyed by the towering Frenchman's "hypersensitiveness and extraordinary stubbornness." But at the same time, he knew that, to many, de Gaulle was the embodiment of French nationalism—as well as the leader who had been given Roosevelt's blessing.

Moreover, Eisenhower now had before him a letter, written by de Gaulle after their last disagreeable meeting and personally delivered by French General Alphonse Juin. It implicitly placed the consequences for failure to seize Paris—a move now necessary "even if it should produce fighting and damage in the interior of the city"—upon Eisenhower. It also renewed the threat to send Leclerc and the French 2nd Armored Division to Paris on their own. Ike had

Masters turned slaves, Germans who once used the Hôtel Majestic as headquarters are forced to clean the streets in front of it after the liberation of Paris. Fences were built to keep Parisians from attacking the Germans.

a feeling that—fuel or no fuel—de Gaulle meant to try exactly that. For the attention of his chief of staff, Lieut. General Walter Bedell Smith, Eisenhower wrote on the letter's margin: "It looks as though we shall be compelled to go into Paris." Whatever doubt remained was dispelled when Bradley and his staff arrived to report Gallois' description of the situation in Paris. "Well, what the hell, Brad," said Ike. "I guess we'll have to go in."

Explaining his reasons for sending troops to Paris, Eisenhower later wrote: "My hand was forced by the actions of the Free French forces inside the city. . . . Information indicated that no great battle would take place and it was believed that the entry of one or two Allied divisions would accomplish the liberation of the city. For the honor of first entry General Bradley selected General Leclerc's French 2nd Division."

Leclerc and Gallois were waiting fretfully on the airstrip at Bradley's headquarters when they first got the word from Sibert. "You win," shouted the intelligence officer as his light plane taxied to a stop. "They've decided to send you straight to Paris." Then, Bradley's plane landed. "The decision has been made to enter Paris," he said quietly, "and the three of us share in the responsibility for it: I, because I have given the order; you, General Leclerc, because you are going to execute it; and you, Major Gallois, because it was largely on the basis of the information you brought us that the decision was made." To Leclerc, Bradley added, "I want you to remember one thing above all. I don't want any fighting in Paris. It's the only order I have for you."

Around dusk, Major General Jacques Leclerc leaped from his plane on the field at Argentan and cried: *"Mouvement immediat sur Paris!"*

Leclerc's drive for Paris started shortly before dawn on Wednesday, August 23, as the French 2nd Armored Division roared out of its bivouac near Ecouché and headed for Paris—slipping and sliding through a lashing rainstorm along winding country roads. The weather could not dampen the ardor of the men, volunteers all, gathered from every corner of the French Empire. There were soldiers from Indochina, Chad, Senegal, Tunisia, Morocco, French Equatorial and Central Africa. Although they were French citizens, most had never been to France until recently, and

Paris was still but a hazy vision. Yet this was the moment they had been waiting for. "A French officer came along and told us we were first for Paris and everybody was tremendously excited," said a soldier. "When we moved off it seemed more like 50 mph than our usual 20."

For his part, Bradley was determined that Leclerc's movement into Paris should not be turned into a triumphant lark. He was aware of the French troops' reputation for being undisciplined—what one American First Army Officer had described as their "casual manner of doing almost exactly what they please, regardless of orders." Therefore, Bradley placed general supervision of the operation under the First Army commander, General Hodges, and gave direct control to the V Corps commander, General Gerow, whose understanding was that he should permit entry into Paris only "in case the degree of fighting was such as could be overcome by light forces."

As the French 2nd Armored set forth, the urgency of its mission was heightened by the delayed appearance at Bradley's headquarters of Rolf Nordling and his strange little delegation from Paris. Nordling's report made it grimly clear that Choltitz could not delay much longer before beginning the demolition of the city. "Tell Hodges to have the French division hurry the hell in there," Bradley ordered one of his staff officers. Then he added, "Tell him to have the 4th Division ready to get in there too. We can't take any chances on that general changing his mind and knocking hell out of the city."

As it happened, a small segment of the U.S. 4th Infantry Division was already on the way to Paris, following the French 2nd Armored, which it had been ordered to assist by seizing the Seine River crossing sites south of the city. Now the rest of the division's troops, veterans of Utah Beach, Cherbourg and the hedgerow fighting in Normandy, began pulling up stakes for the 132-mile trip from Carrouges to Paris.

Although the last thing Leclerc wanted was American (or any other non-French) help, there could be no blinking the fact that his force was making little headway—owing less to enemy opposition than to the weather and to what Bradley later described as a "Gallic wall" of joyously cheering and crowding humanity. Leclerc's orders were to barge straight through Rambouillet and Versailles to Paris. But at Ram-

Carrying badly needed food supplies, Allied planes prepare to land at a Parisian airfield as part of a hastily organized airlift to the French capital. When the Allies liberated Paris on August 25, they discovered that there was only one day's supply of food remaining in the city. On General Eisenhower's orders, planes began shuttling 3,000 tons of food, soap and medical items from Great Britain to Paris at the rate of 500 tons a day.

bouillet, still 30 miles from the capital, he got word that the Germans had moved 60 tanks into the area. On his own authority, he therefore decided to cut 17 miles east to Arpajon and Longjumeau. In doing so, he neglected to inform his American superiors, an omission that, when they heard of it, seemed to confirm their fears about the wayward French.

Meanwhile, de Gaulle had arrived from his temporary command post at Le Mans and had ensconced himself in the magnificent Château de Rambouillet, on the doorstep of Paris, where the leaders of France from Louis XVI to Napoleon had stayed. That night, while the wet, weary men of the 2nd Armored bedded down in nearby woods, Leclerc arrived to confer with his leader. The two discussed Leclerc's battle plan, already being put into effect, and de Gaulle belatedly approved it, virtually without comment. But as Leclerc left, de Gaulle voiced a fear that during these last days had pressed so heavily upon him. "Go fast," he said. "We cannot have another Commune"—a grim refer-

ence to the bloodshed during the Franco-Prussian War in 1871, when Frenchmen, bitterly divided by economic inequalities, had fought one another in the streets of Paris.

Leclerc moved out again at dawn, Thursday, August 24, 1944, aiming three columns toward the southwestern corner of Paris. One column swung west and headed past Versailles, along the route originally assigned to the entire division; its purpose was to draw the enemy away from the main points of attack. A second column thrust through the Chevreuse valley toward Toussus-le-Noble; it would enter Paris through the Porte de Vanves. The third would make the major effort, pushing through the towns of Longjumeau, Antony and Fresnes to strike the capital from the south, at the Porte d'Orléans.

As the three columns slogged forward through a steady drizzle, celebrating throngs continued to slow their progress. Even General Leclerc was caught up in the excitement of the hour. On the way, he stopped in a small town to

telephone his parents in Paris. "Ah, hello, father. This is Philippe," said Leclerc, using the name he had dared not use for the past four years. "I will be calling on you soon and thought you might like to know." When his father asked him where he was, Leclerc replied, "I am just beyond Fontainebleau. I expect it will take me a couple of days to get to Paris, but you can expect me then."

A few hours later, Leclerc's French 2nd Armored ran up against the city's outer defenses, and it appeared that his confident prediction of an early arrival in Paris was in jeopardy. Choltitz had made his final compromise between conscience and military duty: although he would not willingly see Paris destroyed, he would defend its perimeters with everything he had. At Massy-Palaiseau, at Arpajon and at Trappes, some 200 German 88mm guns opened fire on the French columns. Leclerc would have to fight his way into the city.

Meanwhile, at Bradley's headquarters, the American commander was fuming. Leclerc's unannounced change of the attack's axis had taken the French 2nd Armored out of American sight and hearing. As far as Bradley was concerned, the French advance was still being slowed by "wine and celebration. Although I could not censure them for responding to this hospitality of their countrymen, neither could I wait for them to dance their way to Paris." He turned to an aide. "To hell with prestige," he said. "Tell the 4th to slam on in and take the liberation." Later, he would claim that this command had served to spur the French on. "Learning of these orders and fearing an affront to France, Leclerc's troopers mounted their tanks and burned up their treads on the brick roads."

Contrary to Bradley's belief, Leclerc's troops had not been merely liberating and celebrating, nor were they burning up their treads in rapid advance; they were fighting and dying while moving slowly ahead against the concentrated fire. The 88s sliced through the 2nd Armored Division's American-made Sherman tanks. "The firing seemed to go on all day long," said one of Leclerc's men. "The two things most dreaded by our tank crews were the 88s and the Tiger tanks"—some of which the Germans had concealed in haystacks. The French suffered heavy losses on the road to Paris, but they were determined to get there at any cost.

At about 7:30 p.m., Leclerc was still 10 miles from Paris, and he knew it would take at least another 12 hours to enter the city in strength. As he stood at a country roadside, a jeep came to a halt beside him and a red-haired captain jumped out. The jeep had been heading away from Paris, in contravention of Leclerc's orders. "What the hell are you doing here?" snapped Leclerc. Captain Raymond Dronne, the commander of a small tank detachment, was angry too. He

Americans mark the liberation of Paris as the U.S. 28th Division rolls up the Champs-Elysées on August 29, 1944. Though de Gaulle asked for this show of force to strengthen his hand in Paris, the 28th's appearance neatly dovetailed with American battlefield needs. The division moved through the city to the front and took up an attack position the same day.

140

explained that he thought he had discovered a break in the German defenses, but in trying to move through it toward Paris he had twice been ordered back by his commanding officer. "Dronne," said Leclerc, "don't you know enough not to obey stupid orders?" Leclerc pointed his Malacca cane. "I want you to go into Paris," he ordered. "Take whatever you've got and go. Forget about fighting the Germans. Tell them to hold on, we're coming tomorrow."

Dronne had been right about the gap in the German defenses; less than two hours later, at precisely 9:22 p.m., his tank, "Romilly," leading two other Shermans and six half-tracks, arrived at the Hôtel de Ville in the heart of Paris.

Soon after Dronne arrived at the Hôtel de Ville, the bells of Paris—silent for four years—began to ring, first from the south tower of Notre-Dame, then from Sacré-Coeur in Montmartre, then through the length and breadth of the city. Sitting at a candlelit dinner table at the Hôtel Meurice, a young German woman heard the pealing of the bells and turned to her companion. "Why are they ringing?" she asked. "Why are they ringing?" said General von Choltitz. "They are ringing for us, my little girl. They are ringing because the Allies are coming to Paris."

On August 25, Leclerc and his French 2nd Armored Division, closely followed by the U.S. 4th Infantry, entered Paris between 8 and 10:30 a.m. Their arrival touched off one of the most tumultuous celebrations of all time.

In spite of gunfire from Germans and diehard collaborators holding out in some parts of the city, jubilant Parisians poured into the streets to welcome their liberators. They showered the weary and grimy soldiers with champagne and flowers, and smothered them with kisses and hugs. From open windows hung the long-forbidden French tricolor, the Stars and Stripes, the Union Jack and the Soviet hammer and sickle; from the multitudes in the streets rose great cries of delight: *"Vive de Gaulle!" "Vive Leclerc!" "Merci! Merci! Merci!"*

"I have seen the faces of young people in love and the faces of old people at peace with their God. I have never seen in any face such joy as radiated from the faces of the people of Paris this morning," wrote Time war correspondent Charles C. Wertenbaker, who rode into Paris through the Porte d'Orléans at 9:40 a.m. in a jeep directly behind General Leclerc's armored car.

French and American troops reveled in their welcome. They smiled until their faces ached, waved until their arms gave out, shook hands until their hands were bruised and scratched. They drank rivers of wine and champagne proffered by grateful Parisians. War correspondent Ernest Hemingway, accompanying the liberators, arrived in Paris with two truckloads of FFI fighters and headed straight for the Hôtel Ritz bar. There he ordered 73 dry martinis for himself and his companions.

In the meantime, General Leclerc had pushed through the teeming streets, first to the Gare Montparnasse, where he set up his division's headquarters, and then to the Prefecture of Police. There, just as he sat down with Resistance members for a victory luncheon at a table covered with a spotless white cloth, china and flowers, a messenger arrived bringing momentous news. After sharp fighting at the Hôtel Meurice, the German commander of Paris had been captured.

Leclerc got up from the table and went into the next room—the police billiard lounge. Escorted by 20 uniformed policemen, Choltitz entered. "I am General Leclerc," said the Frenchman. "You are no doubt General von Choltitz." Then the two sat down, face to face across a table, and Choltitz signed the surrender of the German forces of Paris. It was 3:00 p.m., August 25, 1944.

Approximately an hour later, Charles de Gaulle rode into Paris in a black Hotchkiss convertible. Inching through the cheering crowds, he went to congratulate Leclerc and his staff at the Gare Montparnasse. Waiting with Leclerc's staff at the station was Colonel Rol. The Communist leader's hopes that his party would fill the vacuum left by the Germans had been dashed by the arrival first of Leclerc, and now of de Gaulle. When the two men came face to face, there was a long, silent pause. Then de Gaulle shook the hand of his rival. From Leclerc's command post, de Gaulle drove a few blocks to establish his headquarters—in the Ministry of War, the same building from which he had fled the Germans four years earlier.

CITY IN REBELLION

Sidewalk superintendents offer words of advice to a Resistance machine gunner in an Henri Cartier-Bresson picture taken during Paris' preliberation revolt.

143

Young Parisians, manning a barricade made out of an overturned truck, watch Cartier-Bresson take their picture from another defense point just down the street from them. The numerous barricades in this area were constructed primarily to guard the central headquarters of the Paris police, seen in the background to the left of the cathedral of Notre-Dame.

A Resistance sharpshooter, under cover in an arcade on the Rue de Rivoli, takes aim at a German making a last-ditch stand on the rooftop of a building across the street. Other FFI fighters wear arm bands bearing the Resistance symbol, the cross of Lorraine, which identified them to fellow patriots but could be discarded quickly if Germans closed in.

Braving heavy German fire, Resistance stretcher-bearers evacuate two wounded women to a first-aid station in nearby Place du Théâtre Français. Parisian casualties during the liberation totaled some 2,300 rebels and 2,600 civilians. The Germans paid a higher price: 7,700 dead or wounded.

White sheets (left), signifying the surrender of Germans inside the Hôtel Continental, are hung out over the Rue de Castiglione, while

148

Parisians gather to watch the mopping-up operations. The German defenders forced the French to clear out the hotel room by room.

Armed with shotguns, gendarmes herd captured German enlisted men past the Louvre to a detention area, where prisoners were registered and sent to POW camps. The first gendarme wears civilian trousers under his uniform jacket, suggesting that he had been fighting for the Resistance and had dressed hastily for his official role after order was restored.

High-ranking German officers wait for the next order from their FFI captors. "Much has been said about how scared the Germans were to be taken prisoner by the FFI," commented Cartier-Bresson, "but really this was exaggerated, as there was no particular violence on the part of the FFI toward the Germans. It came, rather, from the Parisian crowds."

Resistance fighters help themselves to weapons taken from a captured bank that the Germans had used as an arms depot during the Occupation. "The people came for arms as they knew there was a depot," said Cartier-Bresson years later. "I still have an attractive revolver from there."

153

THE TIME OF DELIVERANCE

Exuberant Parisians wave to the soldiers of the French 2nd Armored Division who have come to liberate the French capital on the 25th of August, 1944.

Part of the enthusiastic throng that gathered to welcome de Gaulle waits in vain in the Place de l'Opéra for the general, who took another route.

CHEERING A NEW LEADER

Thousands of Frenchmen watched as de Gaulle marched down the Champs-Elysées on August 26. Cheering civilians lined both sides of the avenue, packed rooftops and windows, climbed up lampposts, flagpoles and trees. One septuagenarian stood atop a ladder 12 feet above the sidewalk.

Few men have known a more supremely satisfying moment of triumph than the one de Gaulle enjoyed now. But the moment was about to be rudely interrupted.

Ecstatic civilians, mingling tears with cheers, greet de Gaulle along the parade

route. As early as 7 o'clock in the morning people had started streaming in from the Paris suburbs on bicycles or on foot to view the 3 o'clock victory parade.

Hundreds of panic-stricken spectators dash for cover as shooting begins in the Hôtel de Ville area, where the de Gaulle party made a stop during the parade.

Close to the cathedral of Notre-Dame, some parents huddle with their frightened children alongside a jeep as a wave of gunfire sweeps through the square.

PANDEMONIUM ON THE AVENUES

As de Gaulle's victory parade headed out of the Champs-Elysées into the Place de la Concorde, a shot suddenly rang out. Thousands of spectators fell to the pavement or scurried to take cover behind the tanks of Leclerc's division. De Gaulle, however, walked indifferently to an open car, which took him to the Hôtel de Ville—Paris' city hall—where he made a brief stop. Then just as he was leaving the Place de l'Hôtel de Ville, machine guns and rifles began rattling from the buildings on the square.

No one knew who started the shooting, but in the street almost every man who had a gun—and hundreds did—started wildly shooting at the windows. Unmoved, de Gaulle rode on to the final stop on his itinerary, the cathedral of Notre-Dame. As he alighted from his automobile, there was more firing. Calmly, the general strode on with the same unhurried, unwavering step into the cathedral.

While shots crackle inside Notre-Dame, de Gaulle sings the "Magnificat."

A FINAL DESPERATE ROUND OF GUNFIRE

When de Gaulle entered the partially darkened cathedral of Notre-Dame, shooting broke out inside the church. The frightened congregation cowered on the floor, prompting André Le Troquer *(above, left)*, one of de Gaulle's ministers, to remark: "I can see more rear ends than faces."

Unruffled, the general moved 190 feet down the aisle to his seat of honor. "He walked straight ahead in what appeared to me to be a hail of fire," a BBC correspondent reported in amazement, "without hesitation, his shoulders flung back. It was the most extraordinary example of courage that I've ever seen."

The shooting persisted, and de Gaulle cut the church service off after the "Magnificat" and quietly left the cathedral. His conduct under fire greatly impressed the people of France. "After that," concluded an American newsman who had watched the general in the cathedral, "de Gaulle had France in the palm of his hand."

A Resistance fighter aims at rooftops near Notre-Dame, hoping to hit unseen

snipers, while a French soldier rushes to take up another firing position. The jittery young gunmen frightened the pedestrians almost as much as the snipers did.

With calm finally settled over the city of Paris, Parisians and newly arrived American soldiers sip wine at a café in Montmartre and attempt to carry on a conversation with the aid of English-French dictionaries.

As the city resumes its normal life, Parisians—photographed through the arch of the Archbishop Bridge—peacefully fish along the banks of the Seine near the

cathedral of Notre-Dame. The liberation accomplished, the majority of the Allied troops moved on to free other parts of France from German domination.

German prisoners were of the same mind, often stating that it couldn't last for another week."

Patton, taking a page from the German book, maintained the blitzkrieg that his Third Army had begun in Normandy. From the right bank of the Seine his forces raced 100 miles, crossing the Marne River and capturing the town of Châlons-sur-Marne. The Germans were unable to organize serious resistance.

On the morning of August 31, in a heavy rain, elements of the Third Army approached the Meuse River at Commercy, 150 miles east of Paris. A light-tank company overran German outposts, knocked out artillery emplacements, seized a bridge and crossed the river. Another column took a bridge-head 10 miles north of Commercy at Saint-Mihiel. Meanwhile, six of Patton's armored columns drove eastward to Epernay, passed Reims, rolled through the Argonne Forest and by noon on August 31 were across the Meuse.

At this juncture, Patton's army was less than 60 miles from the border of Germany. But his supply lines had finally stretched to the breaking point. On the last day of August he had no gasoline at all.

Bitter with frustration, Patton and his staff railed at Eisenhower's decision to give priority on supply to the British Second Army and the U.S. First Army in their drive into Belgium. With no opposition in sight, Patton was forced to park his armor because the gas tanks were dry. To his staff he confided that he faced two enemies—the Germans and his own high command. "I can take care of the Germans," he stormed, "but I'm not sure I can win against Montgomery and Eisenhower.'" His appeals for more gasoline came to no avail. "My men can eat their belts," he bellowed, "but my tanks have gotta have gas."

In the meantime, in the center of the Allies' advance General Hodges' First Army had also made impressive gains. Pushing off from the Seine near Paris and heading northeast, First Army troops rolled back the Germans and liberated the town of Soissons.

At the village of Braine, not far from Soissons, a French railroad stationmaster stopped some American tankers traveling at a fast clip through his town. He told them that a German train was due in 15 minutes. No one listened except Sergeant Hollis Butler of the 3rd Armored Division. His antiaircraft gun section had not fired for several days, and he thought it was time to shoot some live ammunition at a real target, even though it was on the ground.

Pulling his guns out of the column, Butler set them up to cover the railroad. When the train arrived, the crews fired and disabled the locomotive, then turned machine guns on the cars. Advancing in squad formation, Hollis' men captured the 36-car train. French Resistance members appeared to march the German survivors away, and the Americans resumed their advance. From their efforts came a bonus. The stranded train blocked the tracks, and when a second train carrying more Germans pulled into the railroad station a little while later, it was easily captured by an American artillery outfit.

Farther along the way, other elements of the First Army liberated the city of Laon and forged ahead, crossing the Belgian border near Mons and cutting off a mass of Germans, part of the Fifth Panzer Army, fleeing from coastal regions toward their homeland. The German force was strafed by Allied fighter planes and encircled finally by First Army troops. In three days of action some 25,000 Germans were captured. General Hodges, heady with optimism, remarked that with 10 more days of good weather, the war might well be over.

The words were hardly out of Hodges' mouth, however, when he was compelled to curtail his operations. The same hateful problem that had afflicted Patton, the lack of gasoline, forced him to stop one entire corps for three days. His other two corps kept moving, but as they thrust through Luxembourg and Belgium and approached the German border, the advance sputtered fitfully and trucks ran out of gas. Despite its priority on supply, the First Army, like the Third, was coming to the end of its tether.

To the left of the Americans, the British and the Canadian armies had been making great strides in their thrust northward along the French coast. On August 30 elements of the Canadian First Army liberated Rouen, the capital of Normandy. During the first week of September, the Canadians invested the English Channel ports of Le Havre, Boulogne, Calais and Dunkirk, and seized the V-1 launching sites in the Pas-de-Calais.

On the Canadians' right, the British Second Army liberated the city of Amiens on August 31 and captured General

A U.S. tank destroyer fires its 90mm cannon at point-blank range to silence a German pillbox blocking the Allies' path through a Brest street.

BESIEGING BREST'S LAST-DITCH DEFENDERS

The phenomenal speed with which the Allied forces crossed Brittany—200 miles in six days—led them to expect the quick capitulation of their chief target, the port city and German submarine base of Brest. But they did not reckon on the stubbornness of Lieut. General Herman B. Ramcke, commander of some 30,000 crack troops who had been ordered by Hitler to hold out to the last man.

The Germans had turned the city into a huge fortress by constructing elaborate minefields, antitank ditches and concrete dugouts. The Allied troops measured their progress in yards as they took on General Ramcke's 75 strong points, including several old forts, one after another.

On September 18, six weeks after it had begun, the siege ended when the last of the Germans gave themselves up—except for Ramcke, who had escaped. But with nowhere left to go, he surrendered the following day.

Downcast German General Ramcke and his dog are held captive at Allied headquarters.

Eberbach, formerly head of Panzer Group West, now the Seventh Army commander. British armored columns flowed through northern France, rushed across the Belgian frontier and took the capital city of Brussels on September 3. On the next day they took the port of Antwerp, and then, a few days later, the British advance also began to run out of gas. Various units of the Second Army had been dropping out of the pursuit as their vehicles ran dry. Finally, after covering 250 miles in six days, the British advance stopped along the Belgian-Dutch border northeast of Brussels.

In their drive the British had won a major prize, the port of Antwerp. They had seized its wharves and docks before the Germans had had a chance to demolish them. The port's vast capacity was being counted on to ease the Allied logistic crisis, and its nearness to the German border meant that the Allies should not have any problem funneling supplies to their front line.

But Antwerp was to be of no immediate help to the Allies. Its outlet to the sea, the 60-mile Schelde Estuary, was guarded by powerful German forces. So long as the Germans held the banks of this waterway, no Allied ship could run the gauntlet to Antwerp. Yet the British commanders sent no forces to clear the Schelde's banks.

The failure to clear the seaward approaches to Antwerp was attributed later to the sheer exhaustion of the British troops after their long and magnificent drive into Belgium. Another compelling reason, perhaps, was the fact that the attention of the Allied commanders was focused not on Antwerp but on Germany itself. Lieut. General Brian G. Horrocks, commander of the Second Army's XXX Corps, summed up their attitude in his memoirs: "My eyes were entirely fixed on the Rhine and everything else seemed of subsidiary importance."

The first week of September was a time of infectious optimism in the Allied camp. "We have now reached a stage," Montgomery wired Eisenhower on September 4, "where one really powerful and full-blooded thrust toward Berlin is likely to get there and thus end the German war." The Allied Intelligence Committee in London echoed Montgomery's assertion in a report on September 8 that "organized resistance under the control of the German High Command is unlikely to continue beyond December 1, 1944, and it may end even sooner." At that time, the British War Office estimated: "If we go at the same pace as of late, we should be in Berlin by the 28th of September."

There were few dissenters from this rosy view. One who felt otherwise was Colonel Oscar W. Koch, Third Army intelligence chief. Koch warned that the enemy was still capable of a last-ditch struggle. "Barring internal upheaval in the homeland and the remote possibility of insurrection within the Wehrmacht," he wrote, "the German armies will continue to fight until destroyed or captured."

But Koch's minority opinion went unnoticed as optimism swept through all levels of the Allied ranks. The spectacular dash across France, with its brilliant successes against a demoralized enemy, had veiled the commanders' eyes to the reality of the Allied situation. The troops were exhausted. Moreover, their equipment was in need of maintenance,

An American soldier supervises a German prisoner of war as he dismantles a booby trap in a Chartres doorway. Retreating Germans not only booby-trapped objects as small as electric irons but also often employed nonmetal mines that defied detection by conventional methods.

Standing proudly in his jeep, General Patton, commander of the U.S. Third Army, triumphantly crosses a pontoon bridge over the Seine River on August 26, 1944. Later that day, Patton sent a wry message to General Eisenhower to mark the occasion: "Dear Ike: Today I spat in the Seine."

and ceaseless driving had crippled many of their vehicles. Worse, only a trickle of supplies was arriving at the front. The French railway system had been wrecked by air attacks and French Resistance saboteurs.

An Allied innovation called the Red Ball Express, an endless belt of trucks on two parallel one-way routes between Normandy and the forward divisions, proved inadequate to meet the enormous supply demand. The U.S. First and Third Armies required more than 800,000 gallons of gasoline a day. The trucks of the Red Ball Express, operated round the clock, mainly by black service troops, carried great quantities of fuel but burned up an additional 300,000 gallons a day just getting it there.

By the second week of September, after the Allied advance had sputtered, faltered and was crawling to a halt, Allied soldiers began to notice a definite change in the weather. The summer warmth was receding, replaced by frequent rain, fog, mist and cold. Fall was approaching, and winter would not be far behind. Even more alarming were the unmistakable indications of firmer German resistance— a shade more artillery and mortar fire.

The strengthened German defense was no accident. Hit-

ler, shocked into action by the fall of Antwerp, had been taking drastic measures. The foundation of his plan of defense was the West Wall—known to the Allies as the Siegfried Line—a belt of fortifications completed in 1940 that ran along the German border from Switzerland to the Netherlands. Hitler decreed that his forces would fight as long as possible in front of the West Wall, and then pull back and make a stand within the Wall itself, which boasted a formidable array of pillboxes, troop shelters, command posts and tank obstacles.

Early in September Hitler dispatched General Kurt Student to the Belgian-Dutch border to set up defensive positions along the numerous canals that traversed that area.

In what he called "an improvisation on the grandest scale," General Student managed to throw together a makeshift defense, borrowing and confiscating staff, troops and matériel. He was particularly helped by the audacious Major General Kurt Chill, who, retreating with remnants of his own division and two others, had perceived the critical situation along the border, where the British advance threatened. Chill postponed his withdrawal and established straggler collecting points, so that by nightfall of September

4, he had assembled a "crazy-quilt mob" of men from almost every conceivable source. He used them to form a firm line of defense.

To provide a figure around whom his demoralized troops might rally, Hitler recalled from retirement Field Marshal von Rundstedt and appointed the wise old soldier commander in chief in the West. Rundstedt moved quickly and brilliantly to resurrect a protective line along the western approaches to Germany. In one of his first moves, he devised a plan to save the Fifteenth Army, which was trapped in Belgium with its back to the sea.

Following Rundstedt's design, three divisions were left behind to hold the seaward approaches to Antwerp, while 86,000 men of the Fifteenth Army shoved off at night in boats and ferries and crossed the Schelde Estuary to the Beveland peninsula in the German-occupied Netherlands. From there they moved quietly inland down a single road, deep into the Netherlands. Had the British pushed just 15 more miles north after capturing Antwerp, they could have cut the neck of the peninsula and prevented the German escape. But again, because of either exhaustion or short-sightedness, they decided not to press on.

After saving part of the Fifteenth Army, Rundstedt skillfully deployed what units he could pull together in the Netherlands, as well as reserve formations from Germany, against the sputtering advances of the U.S. First and Third Armies. The German units formed a continuous if not altogether solid line from the North Sea to the Swiss frontier.

As the Germans were building up their forces, Montgomery met with Eisenhower in Brussels on September 10 to appeal, once again, for a single massive Allied thrust into Germany. In view of the critical Allied supply situation, Montgomery argued, there simply were not enough resources to keep all the armies pushing forward on a broad front. It would be far more logical, he insisted, to halt Patton's Third Army and the Canadian First Army, giving them just enough supplies to maintain a defensive posture, and to throw full support behind the British Second Army and the American First Army. Those two armies would attack together through the Netherlands and seize the Ruhr. As a preliminary to this main attack, Montgomery laid before Eisenhower a bold and daring scheme, known as Operation *Market-Garden*.

Montgomery proposed dropping three divisions of the Allied First Airborne Army, the Allies' strategic reserve, along a highway connecting the three Dutch cities of Eindhoven, Nijmegen and Arnhem. The airborne troops would seize a series of bridges that spanned canals and three large rivers, clearing the road and holding it open. This phase of the operation was called *Market*. Then, in a coordinated venture called *Garden*, British armored units would dash up the passageway over the bridges and through the cities to link up with the airborne troops. The British tanks would drive 99 miles, all the way to the Zuider Zee, then wheel to the east, outflanking the German West Wall, and go on to seize the Ruhr.

The boldness of this concept startled Montgomery's fellow commanders, who knew him as prudent and meticulous. "Had the pious, teetotaling Montgomery wobbled into SHAEF [Supreme Headquarters, Allied Expeditionary Force] with a hangover, I could not have been more astonished than I was by the daring adventure he proposed," General Bradley later recalled.

Eisenhower was intrigued. Ever since mid-July he had been itching to use his airborne reserve, most of which had dropped into Normandy during the invasion and had thereafter returned to England. Three and a half divisions of paratroopers and glider infantry—the U.S. 82nd and 101st Airborne, the British 1st Airborne and a Polish brigade—were rested, retrained and ready for more action. Eisenhower had asked his planners frequently to find something for the airborne units to do, something, as he put it, "with imagination and daring." Late in August and early in September, the planners had proposed no fewer than 18 different airborne operations. None of them ever got under way, usually because the ground troops, in their hectic dash across France, had overrun the airborne targets before the operations could commence. *Market-Garden* seemed just what he was waiting for.

Furthermore, Eisenhower saw *Market-Garden* as providing the impetus to get the Allies across the Rhine before the supply situation forced another halt and enabled enemy troops to recoup behind the river. Ike again turned thumbs down on Montgomery's demand that he halt the Canadians and the U.S. Third Army in favor of a single thrust by the British and the U.S. First Army, but he gave his approval to

Market-Garden and promised Montgomery sufficient supplies to carry it off.

Having received Eisenhower's approval of the operation on September 10, Montgomery was eager to get started immediately, before the deteriorating weather and a resurgence of German power lessened its chances of success. He picked September 17 as the jump-off date, a deadline that allowed the planners only seven days, hardly enough time to map out such a complex enterprise with thoroughness.

It was obvious to the planners that *Market-Garden* had great potential for failure. Any nagging doubts, however, were soon swept away by the urgency and excitement of planning the largest airborne assault of the war. The Allied commanders were firm in their conviction that the element of surprise would win the bridges and thus ensure a swift passage by the armored column. Behind their optimism lay the assumption that the Germans were incapable of organized resistance. The enemy troops were few, they be-

As everyone pitches in to help out, cans of gasoline bound for Patton's gas-hungry Third Army are unloaded from a C-47 by Air Evacuation Nurse Irene Steffens. Airlifts brought in up to 12,000 gallons a day, a mere trickle in comparison to the 450,000 gallons that Patton required.

lieved, and ill-trained, capable of mustering only a feeble defense. Those Germans could easily be brushed aside.

This belief persisted in the face of disturbing reports to the contrary. Dutch Resistance disclosed that two panzer divisions, the 9th and the 10th SS, battered from their Normandy experience, had stopped in the vicinity of Arnhem to rest and refit. The report was ignored. When the Allies' own intelligence confirmed the Dutch information, Eisenhower's chief of staff, General Smith, deeply concerned about *Market-Garden's* prospects, carried the disquieting report to Montgomery and argued for a revision of the plan. "Montgomery simply waved my objections airily aside," Smith wrote later.

Other evidence of strong German units in the *Market-Garden* area was similarly discounted. The intelligence chief of the British I Airborne Corps, 25-year-old Major Brian Urquhart, laid aerial reconnaissance photos of the Arnhem area on the desk of his superior, Lieut. General Frederick A. M. Browning. Unmistakably, the photos showed German tanks. Browning studied them for a time and told Urquhart not to worry, the tanks were probably in need of repair. After this blithe dismissal of his indisputable evidence, Urquhart's anxiety about *Market-Garden* became so intensified that he was ordered to go on leave. "I had become such a pain around headquarters that on the very eve of the attack I was being removed from the scene," he recalled later. "I was told to go home."

While the Allied armies waited anxiously for ammunition, food and gasoline to come forward, most of the front remained static. On the right flank, elements of General Patch's Seventh Army, which had surged up from the Mediterranean beachhead, made contact with units of Patton's army on September 11, forty miles west of Dijon. With more gasoline at last available, Patton managed to move eastward from the Meuse to grab bridgeheads across the Moselle River, 30 miles from the German border. After foiling a German counterattack, his troops bogged down in the face of increased resistance.

Farther north, on September 11, a First Army patrol in Luxembourg waded across the Our River and set foot on German soil. The soldiers climbed a hill, looked around and returned. Less than a week later, a corps of the First Army crossed into Germany near the border city of Aachen and penetrated the West Wall, but then, overextended and ill-supplied, the unit came to a halt in the face of a fresh German infantry division that had been rushed to the front from East Prussia.

On the coastal flank, the Canadians were inching doggedly toward the Schelde Estuary, Antwerp's yet unopened gateway to the sea, where they would find powerful defenders: three divisions of the Fifteenth Army held there as guardians when the bulk of that army escaped under the noses of the Allies.

All along the extended Allied front, from the North Sea to Switzerland, the American, British, Canadian and French armies were at a virtual standstill. Frustrated by the lack of progress, the Allied high commanders glued their eyes to a single target—the Netherlands—and awaited the onset of Operation *Market-Garden.*

September 17, a Sunday, D-day for *Market-Garden,* dawned hazy but cleared into a beautiful, calm, late summer day with perfect flying conditions. From 24 airfields in Britain, 1,545 C-47s and 478 gliders, protected by 1,131 fighter planes, took to the air and soon were streaming toward their targets: the British 1st Airborne Division to the city of Arnhem, the U.S. 82nd Airborne Division to Nijmegen, the U.S. 101st Airborne Division to the vicinity of Eindhoven.

As the airborne armada neared its drop and landing zones along the 65-mile corridor in the Netherlands, it ran into lighter German opposition than expected. Within a few minutes, 16,500 parachutists and 3,500 glider troops were floating down to earth. Dutch civilians were strolling home from church and sitting down to Sunday dinner when the parachutes, white for soldiers and colored for equipment, blossomed overhead shortly after 1 p.m. "What is it?" a little boy asked his grandfather. "I don't know," the old man said. "But it looks like the end of the war."

The men of the British 1st Airborne Division—the "Red Devils" under Major General Robert E. Urquhart (no relation to Major Brian Urquhart)—came to earth on the north bank of the Lower Rhine, eight miles west of Arnhem and their key objective, the huge highway span over the river in the city. Assembling quickly, they began their march to the bridge, meeting at first almost no opposition.

However, they had gone only a short distance when the

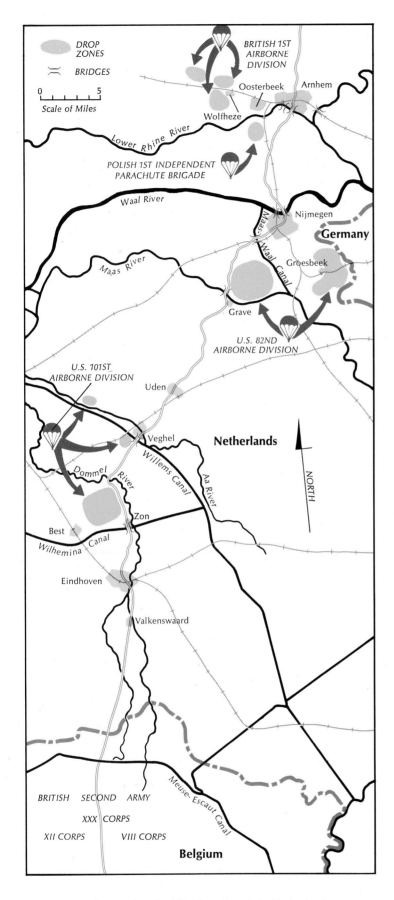

DROP ZONES
BRIDGES

0   5
Scale of Miles

BRITISH 1ST AIRBORNE DIVISION

Oosterbeek   Arnhem

Wolfheze

Lower Rhine River

POLISH 1ST INDEPENDENT PARACHUTE BRIGADE

Waal River

Nijmegen

Germany

Maas River

Groesbeek

Grave

U.S. 82ND AIRBORNE DIVISION

U.S. 101ST AIRBORNE DIVISION

Uden

Veghel   Netherlands

Dommel River   Willems Canal   Aa River

NORTH

Zon

Best

Wilhemina Canal

Eindhoven

Valkenswaard

Meuse-Escaut Canal

BRITISH   SECOND   ARMY

XXX CORPS

XII CORPS   VIII CORPS

Belgium

Operation Market-Garden, the Allied invasion of the Netherlands, began on September 17, 1944, when Anglo-American airborne troops landed near Arnhem, Nijmegen and Eindhoven. They were to seize seven vital bridges and hold open a corridor for tanks of the British Second Army to drive into Germany and bring about an early end to the War.

situation suddenly changed. "One moment we were marching steadily toward Arnhem," recalled Sergeant Major Harry Callaghan, "the next, we were scattered in the ditches. Snipers had opened fire, and three dead airborne soldiers lay across the road."

The sniper fire presaged a more disturbing development. Although they were unaware of it, the British had dropped near a German hornet's nest that was beginning to buzz angrily. As it happened, their drop zones were barely two miles from the headquarters of German Army Group B; its commander, Field Marshal Model, at first thought that the British had launched a daring raid to kidnap him and his staff. Ordering the evacuation of his headquarters, a resort hotel, he leaped into a staff car and raced 18 miles east to the headquarters of Lieut. General Wilhelm Bittrich, commander of the 2nd SS Panzer Corps. He found that Bittrich had already reacted to the invasion—with great foresight, as it turned out.

Bittrich had a hunch that the Allies were bent on forging a bridgehead across the Rhine en route to the Ruhr, and for this they would need the bridges at Arnhem and Nijmegen. He quickly committed his two SS panzer divisions, the 9th and 10th—the very forces whose presence in the *Market-Garden* area the Allied commanders had discounted. Bittrich sent the 9th SS Panzer Division to Arnhem to hold the span across the Lower Rhine. He ordered the 10th Panzer to race to Nijmegen to defend the bridges there.

A couple of hours later, the Germans found a copy of the entire *Market-Garden* plan of operation in a wrecked American glider. The plan included the schedule and locations of reinforcement and supply drops to take place over the next two days. Thanks to that carelessness, the Germans would be ready.

Meanwhile, German troops, bolstered by growing numbers of tanks from the 9th SS Panzer Division, had swiftly cut the main roads over which the British were marching to Arnhem. Consequently, only one unit—the 500 men of Lieut. Colonel John D. Frost's 2nd Battalion, 1st Parachute Brigade—made it to the north end of the bridge.

Frost's men launched an attack across the bridge during the night but were thrown back. The Germans, in force, tried unsuccessfully to bull their way across the bridge from the southern end. Then they brought in troops and laid siege to the British-held houses. Although casualties were increasing and ammunition, food rations and medical supplies were running out, the British refused to give up. They fought savagely from houses and in the streets, waiting for the rest of the 1st Airborne to relieve them.

The rest of the 1st Airborne, however, could not get through to Frost. The Germans had blocked the roads into town, forcing the other two battalions of the 1st Parachute Brigade to make a stand in Oosterbeek, a western suburb of Arnhem. To make matters worse, the division's radio sets, for no apparent reason, were not working.

General Urquhart, desperate for word from Frost, set off for the front with a few members of his staff. They quickly became caught up in the fighting and found themselves surrounded behind German lines. For the next 36 hours, the commander of the 1st Airborne was a fugitive trying to evade capture. He leaped fences in Dutch backyards, lost his way once and hid out in an attic before he finally escaped and made his way to British positions.

While the British situation was deteriorating, the U.S. 82nd Airborne Division, landing in the middle of the *Market-Garden* sector, was moving swiftly to capture a series of bridges in and near the city of Nijmegen. By fortuitous accident, the span at the village of Grave quickly fell into American hands. Above the jump zone near the Maas River bridge south of Nijmegen, the green light in one trans-

port—the signal to leap—flicked on belatedly. When the 16 paratroopers from that plane landed, they found themselves only 600 yards from the bridge. Although the rest of the company was nowhere around, the men, led by Lieutenant John S. Thompson, charged the bridge, spraying it with machine-gun fire. Thompson's men knocked out a flak tower that protected the bridge and quickly overwhelmed the handful of German defenders.

About six miles to the northeast, other paratroopers of the 82nd Airborne grabbed two more bridges, and by the end of the day, only one crucial objective remained in German hands—the highway bridge over the Waal River in the city of Nijmegen. The assault there had been delayed by another mission. Before leading his troops to Nijmegen, the 82nd's commander, Brigadier General James M. Gavin, ordered them to seize and hold a ridge east of the city, the only high ground in the otherwise flat countryside; the rise of land commanded the highway and bridges over which the British ground forces would advance. If the Germans held this position, they could close the highway and choke off the ground assault coming up from the south.

Capturing the height took all afternoon, and it was not until nightfall that Gavin was able to free a battalion to move toward Nijmegen and the division's most important objective, the 1,960-foot bridge over the Waal.

If the 82nd had been able to attack the bridge at the outset, the troops would have found scant opposition. But

The youthful commander of the U.S. 82nd Airborne Division, Brigadier General James M. Gavin, checks his weapons and combat gear before taking off from England for Operation Market-Garden in the Netherlands. The division had been through some of the War's toughest actions in Sicily, Italy and Normandy, but Gavin called the assignment to take the bridge spanning the river at Nijmegen the 82nd's most difficult battle.

An American paratrooper lands upside down in Holland, narrowly missing a haystack that would have softened the blow. During Operation Market-Garden, the largest airborne operation of the War, 35,000 men dropped from planes and gliders. Of these, more than 11,000 were killed, wounded or captured. Many were dead before they hit the ground.

as the light started to fade and the leading company rushed through the streets of Nijmegen heading for the bridge, the first contingents of the 10th SS Panzer Division rolled across the span from the other bank and fanned out against the southern end of the bridge.

An American assault on the bridge that night ended in failure. The next morning, September 18, the men of the 82nd tried again. A company of paratroopers advanced through the back streets, cheered by crowds of Dutch who tossed them fruit and flowers. As the soldiers neared the bridge, the crowds quieted and thinned ominously. Dug in around a traffic circle in a grassy park at the foot of the bridge, the Germans lay in wait. They allowed the Americans to advance to within two blocks of the bridge and then opened up with a machine gun and antiaircraft guns. The paratroopers, ducking from street to street, inched their way to within one block of the bridge and then were stopped.

The Germans clung tenaciously to the bridge, denying the Allies the vital link between the ground forces and the beleaguered paratroopers in Arnhem, 11 miles to the north. American troops at Nijmegen could only await reinforcement from the ground troops advancing up the corridor.

Meanwhile, in the southernmost sector of *Market-Garden*, the U.S. 101st Airborne Division had landed north of Eindhoven and, with great speed and relative ease, seized the village of Veghel and its four rail and highway crossings over the Aa River and the Willems Canal. Then they turned their attention to the south and the vital highway bridge over the Wilhelmina Canal at the village of Zon.

The airborne troops advancing toward Zon met little opposition until they reached the outskirts of town. There, their vanguard came under fire from a German 88mm gun. A bazooka team crept undetected to within 50 yards of the gun and blew it up with one shot. The Americans then ducked and dodged their way forward through the village streets, shooting as they moved along. When they were within a stone's throw of the canal and their objective, a tremendous roar went up and debris rained down on them. The Germans had blown the bridge.

Without hesitation, several paratroopers dived into the canal and swam across, under fire from a house on the far bank. Other American soldiers found a tiny boat, rowed across and quickly subdued the German opposition.

Working feverishly, engineers used lumber brought by Dutch civilians to erect a footbridge across the destroyed span, and a regiment of the 101st walked across in single file. Repairing the bridge for vehicular traffic, however, required heavy equipment that the paratroopers lacked. That would have to wait until the arrival of the ground forces coming up from the Belgian-Dutch border.

Four miles south of Zon, the next morning, September 18, men of the 101st Airborne marched virtually unopposed into Eindhoven to the cheers of the populace. "The recep-

tion was terrific," one soldier noted. "The air seemed to reek with hate for the Germans." Amid the celebration, however, the men of the 101st could not help but notice the conspicuous absence of another contingent in Eindhoven. The British armored column, the thread that was supposed to stitch together the isolated holdings of the three airborne divisions, was nowhere in sight. Expected the previous evening, the ground forces had yet to arrive at Eindhoven.

On the afternoon of September 17, as the paratroopers were landing along the corridor, the British Second Army's XXX Corps moved out of its bridgehead on the Meuse-Escaut Canal and began clanking north up the highway. Its commander, General Horrocks, hoped to adhere to a rigorous timetable: Eindhoven, 13 miles away, by nightfall; Nijmegen, 41 miles farther, by midnight on September 19; and Arnhem, 11 miles farther, by September 21. He realized that his troops faced tremendous hazards. The narrow roadway could accommodate only two tanks abreast. Furthermore, for much of the route, the highway was elevated as it ran across the Dutch flatlands and was thus exposed to enemy observation and gunfire.

Horrocks' worst fears were quickly realized. The Guards Armored Division, the vanguard of the XXX Corps, had scarcely gotten across the Belgian-Dutch border when it ran into a German ambush. German antitank guns that were concealed in the pine woods close to the highway knocked out nine of the Guards' lead tanks, and the advance jarred to a halt. While the British officers fumed at the delay, the British infantry flanking the highway moved forward and cleared out the enemy guns, armored bulldozers pushed the wreckage out of the way, and the column got rolling again. But this first encounter established a pattern that would plague the XXX Corps for another day: a maddening, jerky, stop-and-go progression that would put the advance far behind schedule.

By nightfall of September 17, the ground column was still six miles south of Eindhoven, and not until late in the afternoon of the next day did the British tanks make their way into town—24 hours behind schedule. With crowds of jubilant Dutch civilians their only encumbrance, they moved through Eindhoven to the destroyed bridge at Zon. Working feverishly, British engineers laid a pontoon bridge

across the canal, and the tanks rumbled over it on the morning of September 19, D-plus-2.

From Zon the road north was clear and fast, and the tanks raced to Nijmegen in only a few hours. It began to look as though the operation might pick up sufficient speed to meet the schedule.

But the troops of the 10th SS Panzer Division holding the great highway bridge over the Waal at Nijmegen put an end to any British hopes of regaining the lost time. Firmly entrenched behind coils of barbed wire around the traffic circle at the foot of the bridge, the tough SS troops threw back an attack that afternoon by elements of the Guards Armored and the U.S. 82nd Airborne Divisions. The bridge, the last remaining obstacle in the path to Arnhem just 11 miles away, remained firmly in German hands.

Deeply concerned about the Red Devils at Arnhem, General Gavin proposed a desperate measure to unplug the corridor—an amphibious assault across the Waal in broad daylight. "There's only one way to take this bridge," he told his staff. "We've got to get it simultaneously from both ends." As Gavin conceived the assault, his paratroopers on the south bank would cross the river downstream from the bridge. Gaining the north bank, they would outflank the German position at the bridge and a lesser objective, a railroad bridge. The defenders of both bridges would be overwhelmed. At the same time, the armor from the British ground column would continue to hammer away at the Germans guarding the south end of the highway bridge.

Gavin realized that the river crossing was a gamble. His paratroopers had never tried an operation like it; some had never been in a small boat. But the head-on attacks at the main bridge had been blunted, with heavy casualties, and there seemed to be no practical alternative to a crossing. General Horrocks agreed, and he sent back an order for British boats for the paratroopers. The attack was set for the following day, September 20.

At this juncture of *Market-Garden,* German reinforcements were pouring into the area south of Nijmegen. Elements of the 1st Parachute and Fifteenth Armies, as well as a grab-bag assortment of other German units, stabbed viciously at the British column up and down the corridor, trying to cut the road leading north. The situation reminded Major General Maxwell Taylor of the Old West, "where small garrisons had to contend with sudden Indian attacks at any point along great stretches of vital railroad." His 101st Airborne troops coined a nickname for the 15-mile stretch of road they defended: Hell's Highway.

The Allied reinforcement and supply drops to the British on September 18 and 19 had been a failure. Forewarned of Allied intentions by the captured plans, German troops had overrun some of the drop zones, and bundles of ammunition and food had fallen into their hands.

Clearly, the situation was precarious. And to add to the Allies' anxiety, the commanders had received no word from the 1st Airborne troops at Arnhem. Because of the failure of their radio sets, the Red Devils could not get a message through. An 82nd Airborne intelligence unit did pass along an ominous message from the Dutch underground on September 18: "Dutch report Germans winning at Arnhem."

Allied planners had estimated that the troops at Arnhem could hold out for only four days without relief from the ground forces. On September 20, the fourth day, their fate rested on the outcome of General Gavin's amphibious charge across the Waal. Scheduled for 1 p.m., the assault was delayed because the British boats, held up by traffic jams along the road, had not arrived. They came finally at 2:40 p.m., 33 unwieldy contraptions of plywood and canvas that had to be put together by engineers.

Late in the afternoon, as Allied artillery and British tanks pounded the German defenders on both sides of the river, the first wave of paratroopers, 260 men, led by Major Julian Cook, launched their craft into the strong current of the Waal. Things went wrong from the outset. Some of the flimsy boats flipped over as the soldiers climbed in. Some of them were overloaded and sank. A scarcity of paddles reduced some paratroopers to stroking with their rifle butts. The boats, seized by the current, were swept in circles in the river, out of control.

As the men struggled to steer their craft, the Germans opened up with a hail of machine-gun and mortar fire. From a command post on the river's south side, Lieut. Colonel J. O. E. "Joe" Vandeleur of the Guards Armored watched in awe. "It was a horrible, horrible sight," he recalled. "Boats were literally blown out of the water. Huge geysers shot up as shells hit and small arms fire from the northern bank made the river look like a seething cauldron. I remember almost trying to will the Americans to go faster."

From this maelstrom of fire, about half of the boats emerged finally on the north bank of the river, deposited the survivors and returned for the next wave. Major Cook led the remnants of the assault force across a flat stretch and up an embankment, where they subdued the German defenders in savage hand-to-hand combat. Dashing along the top of the embankment, they gained the northern end of the railroad bridge, trapping a host of German soldiers on the span itself. As the Germans on the bridge tried to escape at the north end, they met concentrated American machine-gun fire. More than 260 were later found dead on the structure, and scores were taken prisoner.

Their numbers swelled by succeeding waves of paratroopers, the Americans then advanced on the highway bridge, their principal objective. At the same time, a British armored attack on the other side of the river finally cracked the German perimeter around the traffic circle at the foot of the span. Through an inferno of burning buildings and shellfire, four British tanks made a wild dash up the bridge approaches and rumbled onto the span. Dueling with German 88mm guns on the bank and machine-gunning the defenders on the span, three made it across the 1,960-foot structure. On the other side, at 7:15 p.m., they met the jubilant U.S. paratroopers who had survived the waterborne assault, an operation that General Horrocks later termed "the most gallant attack ever carried out" in the War.

Arnhem and the battered Red Devils were just 11 miles away. But to the consternation of the American airborne troops, the British armored force halted for the night. The men were weary, and the unit was running low on ammunition and gas. Moreover, the stretch of road to Arnhem offered the worst terrain yet—the road was high, arrow-straight and dangerously exposed. An armored attack down that road would require infantry on the flanks to overcome German resistance, and the British infantry had not yet caught up with the spearhead.

In the heat of the moment, the Americans could not understand why the British tankers did not rush at once to rescue their isolated comrades at Arnhem. "We had killed ourselves crossing the Waal to grab the north end of the bridge," said Colonel Reuben H. Tucker, whose 504th Regiment staged the amphibious operation. "We just stood there seething, as the British settled in for the night, failing to take advantage of the situation. We couldn't understand it. It simply wasn't the way we did things in the American army—especially if it had been our men hanging by their fingernails 11 miles away."

In the meantime, the Red Devils at Arnhem were enduring a hellish German siege. By the end of the second day, September 18, the city around the northern end of the great bridge across the Lower Rhine was littered with wreckage and covered by the stench of battle. Fires raged out of control, and heavy smoke smeared buildings with a greasy black film. Still, Colonel Frost and his dwindling band of paratroopers held out in the houses at the foot of the bridge. Even though they had been surrounded and under constant shellfire, they had not allowed a single German vehicle to cross the span.

Checking his perimeter around midnight on the 18th, Frost discovered that morale was still high among his exhausted and dirty troops. But the basements of the houses they occupied were filled with wounded. They were short of medical supplies and ammunition, and their rations were gone. The paratroopers ate fruit and whatever they could find in the houses.

The German tanks and artillery continued to pound the houses where the paratroopers were holed up through the next day. By the night of September 19, only half of Frost's original 500 men were capable of fighting. At the end of the following day, the number had dwindled to perhaps 150 or 200 men. In the cellars of the shell-pitted houses, the wounded, swathed in filthy bandages, were jammed to-

gether so tightly that medics found it difficult to treat them. Frost himself now lay among them, seriously wounded by an artillery burst.

By the 20th the British had been driven from all but a few of the houses. Most men were down to the last of their ammunition, and Frost concluded that continued resistance was senseless. Shortly before dawn on September 21, he ordered the remnants of his gallant band to try to escape, two or three at a time. Only a few of the remaining 50 men who melted into the darkness got away. Most were captured, including Frost.

A little over two miles away, the rest of the 1st Airborne had been forced back into a U-shaped defensive position, with the open end facing the bend of the Lower Rhine. By September 21 the perimeter had been reduced to a pocket only a mile deep and a mile and a half wide. Into that pocket the Germans poured tons of explosives; so intense was their barrage that they were calling the contested area *Der Hexenkessel*—the witches' cauldron. Pounded mercilessly by the German guns, harassed by German snipers, the 1st Airborne troops nevertheless held out. With little food, water or medical supplies, they waited for the arrival of the ground column, and rescue.

The ground column departed Nijmegen on the morning of September 21, tanks rolling toward Arnhem along the elevated, exposed highway. Six miles short of the Arnhem bridge objective, a single German artillery piece knocked out the lead tanks and stopped the whole column. Once again the operation ground to a halt.

On the afternoon of the same day, the Allies made another effort to reinforce the 1st Airborne. The Polish 1st Independent Parachute Brigade, under the command of

Patients from St. Elisabeth's Hospital in Arnhem are led to safety by a Red Cross worker carrying a white flag. The patients were taken to a town 20 miles away after the hospital came under fire during fighting between German and British troops. The hospital was used by both sides to treat their wounded.

Major General Stanislaw Sosabowski, boarded transports in England for the flight to Arnhem. The Poles were supposed to have jumped into Holland two days earlier, but adverse weather conditions had kept their transports on the ground. In the interim, General Sosabowski, who had been skeptical of *Market-Garden*'s chances to begin with, received sketchy reports that indicated a disaster at Arnhem. Now it seemed to him that his men were being committed to a suicidal effort to redeem a hopeless situation, not to reinforce success as originally intended.

His fears were justified. As the Poles jumped out of their C-47s into an area along the southern bank of the Lower Rhine across from the 1st Airborne perimeter, they floated down into murderous German fire from antiaircraft guns, artillery and small arms. Scores of the descending Polish paratroopers were slain or wounded. The dazed survivors assembled and dug in.

Sosabowski was still intent on reinforcing the Red Devils, however. According to the plan worked out for them, his men were to cross the Lower Rhine by means of a large ferry located on the south bank across from the British perimeter. Shortly after landing, Sosabowski discovered to his dismay that the ferry was nowhere to be found; it had been set adrift by the Germans. Although the Poles later tried to get across the river in a few small boats, German fire forced a halt. There was little Sosabowski could do but await the arrival of the British ground forces from the south.

All day on September 22, D-plus-6, fierce battles raged near Eindhoven and Nijmegen for possession of the *Market-Garden* corridor. That evening a handful of armored cars from the stalled XXX Corps, traveling on back roads, managed to slip through German lines and reach the Polish paratroopers. They were followed by a tank-infantry task force that reinforced Sosabowski's hard-pressed troops.

This was little comfort, however, to General Urquhart and the remaining Red Devils, who continued to fight courageously against superior German forces across the river. By September 24 there were so many British wounded that the makeshift aid stations and Dutch homes in the suburb of Oosterbeek were overflowing. With medical supplies exhausted and the wounded in pitiful condition, Urquhart arranged a truce and turned the injured paratroopers over to the Germans, who held the main hospital in Arnhem.

On the following day, Montgomery, despairing of further attempts to reinforce the Red Devils, finally ordered a withdrawal to save the ragged remains of the division. That night, in a driving rain that helped muffle the noise of movement, the exhausted and numbed survivors quietly left their foxholes. Following guidelines made from parachute tape, or holding hands in a line in the pitch-black darkness, they made their way to the riverbank. As their perimeter gradually thinned out, some of their comrades stayed behind to continue firing and mask the escape.

On the muddy north bank of the Lower Rhine, the Red Devils were met by boats sent up from the XXX Corps and paddled by courageous Canadian and British soldiers. During the night, under sporadic fire by German machine guns, some using tracers, scores of men were ferried to the south bank of the river. The light of dawn revealed to the Germans the extent of the British withdrawal. Still, hundreds of men remained at the river's edge. The Germans began firing, and many of the British plunged into the swift water. Some were swept away by the current or dragged down by the weight of their clothing. Others, as German tanks rumbled unimpeded toward the riverbank, stripped off their clothes and swam across. The remainder, too exhausted or too sick to try to swim, were captured.

The evacuation ended the ordeal of the Red Devils at Arnhem. Of some 10,000 British troops who landed and fought on the north bank of the Lower Rhine, fewer than 2,200 made it back across the river. The British 1st Airborne Division had ceased to exist.

And with the Germans still in possession of the Arnhem bridge, Operation *Market-Garden,* one of the most gallant but disastrous ventures of the War, came to a close. In their bid for a drive into Germany, the Allies had paid a stiff price—17,000 troops dead, wounded or captured.

In one sense *Market-Garden* achieved its objectives. The Allies won a corridor 60 miles long in the Netherlands, and they would continue to hold it. But they had failed to gain a bridgehead over the Rhine or to outflank the West Wall and thus place themselves in position to drive into the Ruhr and on to Berlin. They had been unable to extend their pursuit and bring Germany to collapse. With the failure of *Market-Garden,* the bright Allied vision of a quick end to the War evaporated. A long, hard winter loomed ahead.

THE EMBATTLED BRIDGE

The massive highway bridge at Arnhem, ultimate objective of Operation Market-Garden, lies strewn with debris after the British attempt to take the span failed.

A DARING PLAN TO CROSS THE RHINE

Major General Robert E. "Roy" Urquhart, the commander of the British 1st Airborne Division, stands in front of his headquarters at Arnhem.

On September 17, 1944, as 10,000 men of the British 1st Airborne Division were preparing to take off for German-occupied Holland, a paratrooper named Gordon Spicer remarked that their mission seemed likely to be "a fairly simple affair, with a few backstage Germans recoiling in horror at our approach."

The affair would prove to be anything but simple. The 1st Airborne's objective—the highway bridge over the Lower Rhine at Arnhem—was crucial to the success of the huge Allied operation called *Market-Garden,* the bold but hazardous scheme to get the Allies swiftly across the Rhine and into Germany. Success depended upon two things: the seizure of seven key bridges along a 65-mile corridor in southeastern Holland by Allied paratroopers and glidermen, and the eventual relief of this force by a British armored column driving up from the south.

What Gordon Spicer did not know was that everything had to work to perfection for the operation to succeed. If the narrow corridor designated for the armored column was blocked anywhere along the line, the tanks could be stopped, and the airborne forces beyond that point, cut off from support, would be threatened with annihilation. Pondering the hazards faced by the relieving force, one somewhat more knowledgeable officer observed: "It will be like threading seven needles with one piece of cotton and we only have to miss one to be in trouble."

All such misgivings went unheeded by the Allied planners. When Dutch Resistance sources reported that German panzer formations had moved into the area, their warning was ignored. When Lieut. General Frederick A. M. Browning got a look at the plans, he said to General Montgomery: "I think we might be going a bridge too far." Montgomery paid no attention to Browning.

The bridge that Browning was talking about was the one at Arnhem. Sergeant Walter Inglis of the British 1st Parachute Brigade, in keeping with the general euphoria, told friends the Arnhem bridge would be "a piece of cake." He and his cohorts would find it highly indigestible.

Hands raised in surrender, a British officer disguised as a Dutch civilian in a thwarted attempt to escape capture is questioned by Germans in Arnhem.

rush to unload supplies from Horsa gliders.

The parachute of a British soldier hangs from a tree a few feet away from a camouflaged German tank

In a field near Arnhem, gliders rest at the ends of the trails they scratched in the cultivated earth

PICNICS ON THE WAY TO A BLOODY BATTLE

After the paratroopers had landed, Lieut. Colonel John D. Frost, colorful commander of the 2nd Battalion of the 1st Parachute Brigade, rallied his men with a hunting horn and led them onto a secondary road to Arnhem. They were charged with making a quick dash to the city to seize the bridge while the 1st and 3rd Battalions, following main roads, were to come in behind them and occupy the city and high ground to the north.

As the three battalions moved toward Arnhem, they encountered an unexpected hazard: the Dutch they were liberating. "Waving, cheering, and clapping their hands," a battalion officer later recount-

ed, "they offered us apples, pears, something to drink. But they interfered with our progress and filled me with dread that they would give our positions away."

The Germans were quick to take advantage of the British soldiers' predicament. "One moment we were marching steadily toward Arnhem; the next, we were scattered in the ditches," recalled one officer. "Snipers had opened fire, and three dead airborne soldiers lay across the road."

As the enemy fire intensified, the 1st and 3rd Battalions bogged down. But Frost and his men, pushing along a lightly guarded secondary road, made it through to the city, and in the fading light of dusk they reached the northern end of the bridge. They moved quietly into buildings nearby and set up a base of operations for an attack on the span.

Checking the supplies in its jeep, a patrol led by a glider pilot—in the kilt he was wearing when he landed—prepares to move toward Arnhem. Jeep patrols set out first to scout the roads that the airborne troops would use.

Pausing for a moment on their push to Arnhem
two British soldiers enjoy an impromptu picnic
provided by a grateful Dutch girl. British leaders
found that the crowds of joyous civilians
made it very difficult for their troops "to keep
alive to the possibility of a German attack."

As Dutch civilians look on, British troops
round up stray German soldiers near Arnhem.
Earlier, when retreating Germans had poured
through Arnhem on their way to Germany,
the emboldened Dutch taunted them with
scornful shouts of "Go home. The British and
Americans will be here in a few hours."

German soldiers dash across a rubble-cluttered street in Arnhem (left), while British paratroopers cautiously advance through the ruins of a house (right).

Braced against a window sill, a British soldier takes aim at a target in the street (left). At right, German troops leap over a fence to take up new positions

Enjoying some wine and a smoke, well-equipped Germans seem unconcerned by the British attack.

Alerted to the British invasion, Germans in a self-propelled gun patrol a tree-lined street in Arnhem.

German troops creep forward around a British tank.

A NEVER-ENDING WAIT FOR REINFORCEMENTS

While the Germans mercilessly pounded them, the tired, dogged men of the British 1st Airborne were sustained by one thought—airdrops would bring relief.

But the Germans closed in on the drop zones and greeted transports and gliders with hailstorms of mortar and antiaircraft fire. Some glider pilots, trying to escape the enemy barrage, released their planes too soon. The flimsy craft collided in midair and plowed into one another on the ground. Transports burst into flames and crashed; others—even though they were on fire—continued to hover over the drop zones. A doomed Dakota made repeated drops after its lower fuselage was engulfed in flames. An awestruck British officer who watched from the ground recalled later, "I couldn't take my eyes off the craft. Suddenly it wasn't a plane anymore, just a big orange ball of fire."

Most of the supplies fell behind German lines. In two days of drops, the enemy captured nearly 630 of the 690 tons of supplies that had been intended for the beleaguered airborne troops. "It was the cheapest battle we ever fought," said one German colonel. "We had free food, cigarettes and ammunition."

Even more disastrous for the British at Arnhem was the inability of the 1,500 men of the Polish 1st Independent Parachute Brigade to reach them. Grounded in England for two days by bad weather, the brigade finally took off on the afternoon of September 21. As the planes flew over Holland, the brigade commander, Major General Stanislaw Sosabowski, staring out of the window of his Dakota transport, saw huge traffic jams, burning vehicles and wreckage on the road north of Eindhoven. This could mean only one thing: the British relief column coming up from the south was under heavy German attack.

Sosabowski's sagging spirits received another jolt shortly afterward, when he spotted German tanks on the Arnhem bridge: obviously, the British paratroopers had not taken their main objective. Sosabowski bitterly concluded that his brigade was "being sacrificed in a complete British disaster." Moments later, as the Polish troops began to bail out over the drop zone, they were cut to pieces by German antiaircraft fire. Only half of them ever made it to Arnhem, and they arrived there too late to do much good.

British soldiers near Arnhem, exhausted by days of continuous fighting, anxiously await supply drops

Polish paratroopers, who were to reinforce the British, wait in England to board planes for Arnhem

Urgently needed supplies for British troops float down to drop zones near Arnhem. Unknown to the plane crews, Germans had already overrun the zones

Frantically waving table linen taken from a nearby hotel, British soldiers on the edge of a drop zone try to attract the attention of supply planes overhead

Shattered houses from which the British fought indicate the force of the German tank and artillery attack. The shellfire was so relentless that one German soldier

ZEROING IN ON
THE RED DEVILS

At the bridge, Frost's men had managed to hold on for almost 72 hours. But then German tanks and artillery, working in relays,

started systematically blasting the British positions. "It was the best, most effective fire I have ever seen," recalled a German private. "Starting from the rooftops, buildings collapsed like doll houses."

Frost ordered those who could to escape and then arranged a truce with the Ger-

mans to remove the injured. One of the wounded was Frost himself. As he was carried out on a stretcher, he said to the man lying next to him, "Well, we didn't get away with it this time, did we?" "No, sir," answered the man, "but we gave them a damn good run for their money."

... later admitted "I truly felt sorry for the British."

The bullet-riddled corpse of a German soldier lies where he fell from a car after a British attack

The crumpled bodies of two British soldiers rest next to a taunting milestone on a road to Arnhem

A British soldier wears a ragtag outfit assembled after he swam the Rhine.

TRAGIC COST OF
A MISSION THAT FAILED

On the night of September 25, all hopes
for reinforcement gone, the battered remnants of the British 1st Airborne Division
began a quiet withdrawal under the noses
of the Germans. Their feet wrapped up in
cloth to muffle the sound of their boots,
the survivors of the ill-fated operation fil-
tered through the darkness to the north
bank of the Lower Rhine and later were
ferried or swam to safety. The division had
lost 7,500 of its original 10,000 men.

But, said General Eisenhower afterward:
"No single performance by any unit . . .
more highly excited my admiration."

close watch of his Ge   captors   British prisone

his contempt with a snarl and a gesture. One officer who recalled watching his men retreat remarked, "By God we had come out as we went in. Proud."

BIBLIOGRAPHY

Adelman, Robert H., and Colonel George Walton, *The Champagne Campaign*. Little, Brown and Co., 1969.

Amouroux, Henri, *La Vie des Français sous l'Occupation*, Vol. 1. Fayard, 1961.

Aron, Robert, *France Reborn: The History of the Liberation, June 1944–May 1945*. Charles Scribner's Sons, 1964.

Barber, Noel, *The Week France Fell: June 1940*. Macmillan London Ltd., 1976.

Baudot, Marcel, *Libération de la Normandie*. Librairie Hachette, 1974.

Bradley, Omar N., *A Soldier's Story*. Henry Holt and Co., 1951.

Buisson, Doctors Jules and Gilles, *Mortain et sa Bataille, 2 August–13 August 1944*. Imprimerie Maurice Simon, 1947.

Bullock, Alan, *Hitler: A Study in Tyranny*. Harper & Row, 1971.

Butcher, Captain Harry C., USNR, *My Three Years with Eisenhower*. Simon and Schuster, 1946.

Carell, Paul, *Invasion—They're Coming!* E. P. Dutton & Co., Inc., 1963.

Carr, William Guy, *Checkmate in the North: The Axis Planned to Invade America*. The Macmillan Company of Canada Ltd., 1944.

Carter, Ross S., *Those Devils in Baggy Pants*. Appleton-Century-Crofts, Inc., 1951.

Cartier-Bresson, Henri, *The World of Henri Cartier-Bresson*. The Viking Press, 1968.

Churchill, Winston S.:
The Second World War. Houghton Mifflin Co.
Vol. 5, *Closing the Ring*, 1951.
Vol. 6, *Triumph and Tragedy*, 1953.

Collins, Larry, and Dominique Lapierre, *Is Paris Burning?* Simon and Schuster, 1965.

Commission du Coût de l'Occupation, *Evaluation des Dommages Subis par la France: du fait de la Guerre et de l'Occupation Ennemie (1939-1945)*. Institut de Conjoncture, no date.

Cooke, David C., and Martin Caidin, *Jets, Rockets and Guided Missiles*. The McBride Co., 1951.

Craven, Wesley Frank, and James Lea Cate, eds., *The Army Air Forces in World War II*, Vol. 3, *Europe: Argument to V-E Day (January 1944 to May 1945)*. The University of Chicago Press, 1951.

Dank, Milton, *The French against the French: Collaboration and Resistance*. J. B. Lippincott Co., 1974.

Dawidowicz, Lucy S., *The War against the Jews 1933-1945*. Holt, Rinehart and Winston, 1975.

De Gaulle, Charles, *The Complete War Memoirs of Charles de Gaulle*. Simon and Schuster, 1972.

De La Ferte, Air Chief Marshal Sir Philip Joubert, *Rocket*. Philosophical Library, Inc., 1957.

Dornbusch, C. E.:
compiler, *Histories of American Army Units, World Wars I and II and Korean Conflict*. Special Services Division, Office of the Adjutant General, Department of the Army, 1956.
Histories: Personal Narratives, United States Army (A Checklist). Hope Farm Press, 1967.

Douglas, W. A. B., and Brereton Greenhous, *Out of the Shadows*. Oxford University Press, 1977.

Downing, David, *The Devil's Virtuosos: German Generals at War 1940-5*. St. Martin's Press, 1977.

DuJardin, Raoul, *Les Routes sans Oiseaux*. Flammarion, 1947.

Eisenhower, Dwight D., *Crusade in Europe*. Doubleday & Co., Inc., 1948.

Ellis, Major L. F., *Victory in the West*, Vol. 1, *The Battle of Normandy*. Her Majesty's Stationery Office, 1962.

Eparvier, Jean, *A Paris sous la Botte des Nazis*. Editions Raymond Schall, 1944.

Esposito, Brig. General Vincent J., USA (Ret.), chief ed., *The West Point Atlas of American Wars*, Vol. 2, *1900-1953*. Frederick A. Praeger, 1959.

Essame, H., *Patton: A Study in Command*. Charles Scribner's Sons, 1974.

Florentin, Eddy, *The Battle of the Falaise Gap*. Hawthorne Books, Inc., no date.

Flower, Desmond, and James Reeves, eds., *The Taste of Courage: The War, 1939-1945*. Harper & Brothers, 1960.

Gavin, Major General James M.:
Airborne Warfare. Infantry Journal Press, 1947.
On to Berlin: Battles of an Airborne Commander 1943-1946. The Viking Press, 1978.

Gosset, André, and Paul LeComte, *Caen: pendant la Bataille*. Ozanne et C., no date.

Grall, Jeanne, *1944: La Libération du Calvados en Images*. S.P.R.L. SODIM, 1977.

Greenfield, Kent Roberts, ed., *Command Decisions*. Office of the Chief of Military History, Department of the Army, 1960.

Haupt, Werner, *Rückzug im Westen 1944*. Motorbuch Verlag, 1978.

Howard, Michael, *Grand Strategy*, Vol. 4, *August 1942-September 1943*, History of the Second World War, United Kingdom Military Series, edited by J. R. M. Butler. Her Majesty's Stationery Office, 1972.

Huddleston, Sisley, *France: The Tragic Years 1939-1947*. The Devin-Adair Co., 1955.

Huston, James A., *Across the Face of France: Liberation and Recovery 1944-63*. Purdue University Studies, 1963.

Jane, Fred T., *Jane's All the World's Aircraft 1945/6*. David & Charles Ltd., 1970.

Johnson, Brian, *The Secret War*. British Broadcasting Corporation, 1978.

Jones, R. V., *Most Secret War*. Hamish Hamilton Ltd., 1978.

Kay, Anthony L., *Monogram Close-Up 4—Buzz Bomb*. Monogram Aviation Publications, 1977.

Kernan, Thomas D., *Report on France*. John Lane, 1942.

Kesselring, Albert, *Kesselring: A Soldier's Record*. William Morrow & Co., 1954.

Lang, Will, "Lucian King Truscott, Jr." LIFE, October 2, 1944.

Lantier, Maurice, *Saint-Lô au Bucher*. Imprimerie Jacqueline, no date.

Le Boterf, Hervé, *La Vie Parisienne sous l'Occupation: 1940-1944*, Vol. 1. Editions France-Empire, 1974.

LeFrançois, Auguste-Louis, *Quand Saint-Lô Voulait Revivre: Juillet à Noël 1944*. Imprimerie P. Bellée, no date.

MacDonald, Charles B., *Airborne*. Ballantine Books Inc., 1970.

McKee, Alexander, *Last Round against Rommel: Battle of the Normandy Bridgehead*. The New American Library, 1964.

Majdalany, Fred, *The Fall of Fortress Europe*. Hodder and Stoughton Ltd., 1968.

Manvell, Roger, *SS and Gestapo: Rule by Terror*. Ballantine Books Inc., 1969.

Matloff, Maurice, *United States Army in World War II, The War Department, Strategic Planning for Coalition Warfare: 1943-1944*. Office of the Chief of Military History, Department of the Army, 1959.

Maule, Henry:
Normandy Breakout. Quadrangle/The New York Times Book Co., 1977.
Out of the Sand: The Epic Story of General Leclerc and the Fighting Free French. Odhams Books Ltd., 1966.

Mellenthin, F. W. von, *German Generals of World War II: As I Saw Them*. University of Oklahoma Press, 1977.

Michael [pseud.], *France Still Lives*. Lindsay Drummond, 1942.

Montgomery of Alamein, Field-Marshal the Viscount, *The Memoirs of Field-Marshal the Viscount Montgomery of Alamein, K.G.* The World Publishing Co., 1958.

Monzein, A. and P., and Y. Chapron, *A la Charnière (Caen 1944)*. Flammarion, 1947.

Moorehead, Alan, *Eclipse*. Harper & Row, 1968.

Moran, Lord, *Churchill—Taken from the Diaries of Lord Moran—The Struggle for Survival 1940-1965*. Norman S. Berg, 1976.

Mordal, Jacques, *La Bataille de France 1944-1945*. B. Arthaud, 1964.

Morison, Samuel Eliot, *History of United States Naval Operations in World War II*, Vol. 11, *The Invasion of France and Germany 1944-1945*. Little, Brown and Co., 1975.

Piekalkiewicz, Janusz, *Arnhem 1944*. Charles Scribner's Sons, 1976.

Pogue, Forrest C., *George C. Marshall: Organizer of Victory—1943-1945*. The Viking Press, 1973.

Polnay, Peter de, *The Germans Came to Paris*. Duell, Sloan and Pearce, 1943.

Porter, Roy P., *Uncensored France*. The Dial Press, 1942.

Powley, A. E., *Broadcast from the Front (Canadian Radio Overseas in the Second World War)*. Hakkert, 1975.

Pyle, Ernie, *Brave Men*. Henry Holt and Co., 1944.

Renaudot, Françoise, *Les Français et l'Occupation*. Editions Robert Laffont, 1975.

Report of Operations: The Seventh United States Army in France and Germany 1944-1945, Vol. 1. Aloys Gräf, 1946.

Robichon, Jacques, *The Second D-Day*. Walker and Co., 1969.

Ryan, Cornelius, *A Bridge Too Far*. Popular Library, 1974.

St-Lô (7 July-19 July 1944), American Forces in Action Series. Historical Division, War Department, 1946.

Saunders, Hilary St. George, *Royal Air Force 1939-1945*, Vol. 3, *The Fight is Won*. Her Majesty's Stationery Office, 1975.

Sosabowski, Major-General Stanislaw, *Freely I Served*. William Kimber, 1960.

Stacey, Colonel C. P.:
The Canadian Army at War: Canada's Battle in Normandy. King's Printer, 1946.
The Canadian Army 1939-1945: An Official Historical Summary. King's Printer, 1948.
Not in Vain. University of Toronto Press, 1973.
Official History of the Canadian Army in the Second World War, Vol. 3, *The Victory Campaign (The Operations in North-West Europe 1944-1945)*. The Queen's Printer and Controller of Stationery, 1960.

Taggart, Donald G., *History of the Third Infantry Division in World War II*. Infantry Journal Press, 1947.

Tassigny, Marshal de Lattre de, *The History of the French First Army*. George Allen and Unwin Ltd., 1952.

Thompson, Robert Smith, *Pledge to Destiny—Charles de Gaulle and the Rise of the Free French*. McGraw-Hill Book Co., 1974.

Thornton, Willis, *The Liberation of Paris*. Harcourt, Brace & World, Inc., 1962.

Truscott, Lieut. General L. K., Jr., *Command Missions: A Personal Story*. E. P. Dutton and Co., Inc., 1954.

United States Army in World War II, The European Theater of Operations. Office of the Chief of Military History, Department of the Army:
Blumenson, Martin, *Breakout and Pursuit*, 1961.
Cole, Hugh M., *The Lorraine Campaign*, 1950.
MacDonald, Charles B., *The Siegfried Line Campaign*, 1963.
Pogue, Forrest C., *The Supreme Command*, 1954.
Ruppenthal, Roland G., *Logistical Support of the Armies*, 2 vols., 1959.

Urquhart, Major-General R. E., *Arnhem*. W. W. Norton & Co., Inc., 1958.

Vigneras, Marcel, *United States Army in World War II, Special Studies: Rearming the French.* Office of the Chief of Military History, Department of the Army, 1957.
Walter, Gérard, *Paris under the Occupation.* The Orion Press, 1960.
Warlimont, Walter, *Inside Hitler's Headquarters 1939-1945.* Frederick A.
Praeger, 1964.
Werth, Alexander, *France 1940-1955.* Henry Holt and Co., 1956.
Whitcombe, Fred, ed., *The Pictorial History of Canada's Army Overseas 1939-1945.* Whitcombe, Gilmour & Co., 1947.
Wilmot, Chester, *The Struggle for Europe.* Harper & Brothers, 1952.

ACKNOWLEDGMENTS

The index for this book was prepared by Mel Ingber. For help given in the preparation of this book the editors wish to express their gratitude to Gérard Baschet, Editions de l'Illustration, Paris; Dana Bell, U.S. Air Force Still Photo Depository, Pentagon, Washington, D.C.; Leroy Bellamy, Prints and Photographs Division, Library of Congress, Washington, D.C.; Georges Bidault, Paris; Léon Bonin, Paris; Carole Boutté, Senior Researcher, U.S. Army Audio-Visual Activity, Pentagon, Washington, D.C.; Henri Cartier-Bresson, Paris; Huguette Chalufour, Editions Jules Taillandier, Paris; Yves Ciampi, Paris; Charles de Coligny, Curator, Musée de l'Ordre de la Libération, Paris; Cécile Coutin, Curator, Musée des Deux Guerres Mondiales, Paris; Cécile Dabosville, Les Moutiers-en-Cinglais, France; Mrs. Charles de Gaulle, Colombey-les-Deux-Eglises, France; Patrick Dempsey, Geography and Map Division, Library of Congress, Alexandria, Virginia; V. M. Destefano, Chief, Reference Library, U.S. Army Audio-Visual Activity, Pentagon, Washington, D.C.; Ken Dillon, Alexandria, Virginia; Robert Doisneau, Paris; Hans Dollinger, Wörthsee, Germany; Colonel Marcel Dugué-MacCarthy, Curator, Musée de l'Armée, Paris; Georges Févre, Paris; General James M. Gavin, Cambridge, Massachusetts; Dr. Paul German, Falaise, France; Government Institute for War Documentation, Amsterdam; Jeanne Grall, Curator, Archives Municipales, Caen, France; Nelly Guicheteau, Paris; Dr. Robert Guillermou, Evreux, France; Robert and Jeanne Halley, Caen, France; Al Hardin, The Army Library, Pentagon, Washington, D.C.; MacDonald Hastings, London; Dr. Matthias Haupt, Bundesarchiv, Koblenz, Germany; Werner Haupt, Bibliothek für Zeitgeschichte, Stuttgart, Germany; Thierry Hollier-Larousse, Le Mesnil-de-Louvigny, France; Roger Huguen, Saint-Brieuc, France; Jerry Kearns, Prints and Photographs Division, Library of Congress, Washington, D.C.; Lawrence Kennedy, Franconia, Virginia; Dr. Roland Klemig, Bildarchiv Preussischer Kulturbesitz, Berlin; Gene Kubal, The Army Library, Pentagon, Washington, D.C.; William H. Leary, National Archives and Records Service, Audio-Visual Division, Washington, D.C.; André Lebrun, Caen, France; Auguste Lefrancois, Saint-Lô, France; Donald S. Lopez, Assistant Director of Aeronautics, The National Air and Space Museum, The Smithsonian Institution, Washington, D.C.; Leonard McCombe, Long Island, New York; Major Mike Mandel, Chief of Photojournalism Branch, Office of the Chief of Public Affairs, Pentagon, Washington, D.C.; Colonel Jean Martel, Curator, Musée de l'Armée, Paris; Brün Meyer, Bundesarchiv, Freiburg, Germany; Henri Michel, President, Comité d'Histoire de la Deuxième Guerre Mondiale, Paris; Claude Monnerat, I.N.R.P., Paris; Municipal Museum, Nijmegen, The Netherlands; General Sir Richard O'Connor, D.S.O., M.C., London; Thomas Oglesby, National Archives and Records Service, Audio-Visual Division, Washington, D.C.; Emile Perez, Paris; Raoul Pérol, Institut Charles de Gaulle, Paris; Yves Perret-Gentil, Comité d'Histoire de la Deuxième Guerre Mondiale, Paris; Janusz Piekalkiewicz, Rösrath-Hoffnungsthal, Germany; Dr. Etienne Poilpré, Mathieu, Paris; Marianne Ranson, Comité d'Histoire de la Deuxième Guerre Mondiale, Paris; Michel Rauzier, Comité d'Histoire de la Deuxième Guerre Mondiale, Paris; John Riley, Special Projects Historian, Ships' Histories Branch, Naval Historical Center, Navy Yard, Washington, D.C.; Axel Schulz, Ullstein Bilderdienst, Berlin; Joseph Thomas, National Archives and Records Service, Audio-Visual Division, Washington, D.C.; Dominique Veillon, Comité d'Histoire de la Deuxième Guerre Mondiale, Paris; Dr. Jean Verdier, Sainte-Maxime, France; Chuck Vinch, Office of the Chief of Public Affairs, Pentagon, Washington, D.C.; Paul White, National Archives and Records Service, Audio-Visual Division, Washington, D.C.; Colonel Paul Willing, Curator, Musée de l'Armée, Paris; Marjorie Willis, Radio Times Hulton Picture Library, London; Marie Yates, U.S. Army Audio-Visual Activity, Pentagon, Washington, D.C. Particularly valuable sources for this book were: *Normandy Breakout* by Henry Maule, Quadrangle/The New York Times Book Company, 1977; and *Brave Men* by Ernie Pyle, Henry Holt and Company, 1944.

PICTURE CREDITS
Credits from left to right are separated by semicolons, from top to bottom by dashes.

COVER and page 1: Robert Capa from Magnum.

PARIS UNDER THE SWASTIKA—6, 7: Zucca/Tallandier from Magnum. 8: Zucca © Tallandier, Paris. 9, 10: Zucca/Tallandier from Magnum. 11: Zucca © Tallandier, Paris. 12, 13: Zucca/Tallandier from Magnum (2); Zucca © Tallandier, Paris. 14, 15: Bundesarchiv, Koblenz; Zucca/Tallandier from Magnum.

BATTLE OF THE HEDGEROWS—18, 19: Map by Elie Sabban. 21: Ministère de l'Equipement, Institut Géographique National, Paris—Wide World—UPI. 23: U.S. Army. 25: Radio Times Hulton Picture Library, London. 26: Ullstein Bilderdienst, Berlin—Bundesarchiv, Koblenz. 29: Frank Scherschel for LIFE.

SHAMBLES AT CHERBOURG—32, 33: U.S. Army. 34: National Archives. 35: U.S. Army. 36: National Archives. 37: U.S. Army, except bottom left, National Archives. 38, 39: U.S. Army (2); David E. Scherman for LIFE. 40, 41: U.S. Army. 42: National Archives. 43: U.S. Army. 44, 45: National Archives—U.S. Army; David E. Scherman for LIFE.

BREAKOUT—49: UPI. 50: Süddeutscher Verlag, Bilderdienst, Munich. 51: Wide World, courtesy Imperial War Museum, London. 52: Wide World. 53: U.S. Army. 55, 56: Wide World. 57: Map by Elie Sabban. 58: U.S. Air Force.

CAUGHT IN THE CROSS FIRE—60, 61: Ullstein Bilderdienst, Berlin. 62: Radio Times Hulton Picture Library, London. 63: U.S. Army. 64, 65: Top right, Wide World—Imperial War Museum, London. 66 through 69: Leonard McCombe from Radio Times Hulton Picture Library, London. 70, 71: Imperial War Museum, London; U.S. Army (2)—Imperial War Museum, London; George Rodger for LIFE; Imperial War Museum, London. 72, 73: Bob Landry for LIFE; National Archives—U.S. Army. 74, 75: UPI; U.S. Army.

THE GERMANS ON THE RUN—79: UPI. 80: Map by Elie Sabban. 83: Imperial War Museum, London; Ullstein Bilderdienst, Berlin.

AN AMERICAN BLITZKRIEG—86, 87: U.S. Army. 88: U.S. Army—Map by Elie Sabban. 89: U.S. Army. 90, 91: Photo Delaunay-Huguen, Saint-Brieuc—Map by Elie Sabban; U.S. Army. 92 through 97: U.S. Army, except maps by Elie Sabban. 98, 99: U.S. Army—Map by Elie Sabban; Ralph Morse for LIFE.

SOUTHERN FRANCE'S D-DAY—102: Map by Elie Sabban. 106: UPI. 109, 111: E. C. P. Armées, Paris. 113: U.S. Army.

THE PARISIANS MASTER WAR—116, 117: H. Roger-Viollet, Paris. 118, 119: © Almasy, Paris. 120, 121: H. Roger-Viollet, Paris; Photo Seeberger, Paris. 122: Collection Comité d'Histoire de la Deuxième Guerre Mondiale, Paris. 123, 124: Photo Robert Doisneau-Rapho, Paris. 125: Photo Seeberger, Paris (2)—Bibliothèque Nationale, Paris. 126, 127: H. Roger-Viollet, Paris; Roger Schall, Paris.

A DIABOLICAL PLAN THWARTED—130: Office of War Information photo by Weston Haynes, courtesy Imperial War Museum, London. 133 through 140: U.S. Army.

CITY IN REBELLION—142 through 153: Henri Cartier-Bresson.

THE TIME OF DELIVERANCE—154, 155: H. Roger-Viollet, Paris. 156: Photo Lapi, Musée de la Préfecture de Police, Paris. 157: Robert Capa for LIFE. 158, 159: Léon Bonin, Musée de la Préfecture de Police, Paris; U.S. Army. 160, 161: Frank Scherschel for LIFE; Rapho, Paris—UPI. 162, 163: Robert Capa from Magnum. 164, 165: Frank Scherschel for LIFE; Ralph Morse for LIFE. 166, 167: U.S. Army, courtesy Imperial War Museum, London; Ralph Morse for LIFE. 168, 169: Frank Scherschel for LIFE.

NIGHTMARE IN HOLLAND—173 through 177: U.S. Army. 179: Map by Elie Sabban. 180: U.S. Army, courtesy James M. Gavin. 181: U.S. Army. 184: Bundesarchiv, Koblenz.

THE EMBATTLED BRIDGE—186, 187, 188: Imperial War Museum, London. 189: Süddeutscher Verlag, Bilderdienst, Munich. 190, 191: Government Institute for War Documentation, Amsterdam, copied by Martin Vries; Imperial War Museum, London (2). 192: Imperial War Museum, London. 193: Imperial War Museum, London—Government Institute for War Documentation, Amsterdam. 194: Bundesarchiv, Koblenz; Imperial War Museum, London—Imperial War Museum, London; Bundesarchiv, Koblenz. 195: Imperial War Museum, London. 196, 197: Bundesarchiv, Koblenz (2); Imperial War Museum, London. 198: Imperial War Museum, London—Janusz Piekalkiewicz, Rösrath-Hoffnungsthal. 199: Government Institute for War Documentation, Amsterdam—Janusz Piekalkiewicz, Rösrath-Hoffnungsthal. 200, 201: Government Institute for War Documentation, Amsterdam; Imperial War Museum, London—Bundesarchiv, Koblenz. 202, 203: Imperial War Museum, London; Bundesarchiv, Koblenz.

INDEX

*Numerals in italics indicate an illustration
of the subject mentioned.*